MINERS STRIKE

1984-1985

People versus State

David Reed and Olivia Adamson

Larkin Publications

©Larkin Publications 1985

Larkin Publications
BCM Box 5909 London WC1N 3XX

First published in 1985

British Library in Publication Data

Reed, David
 Miners strike 1984-1985: people versus state.
 1. Coal strike, Great Britain, 1984-1985
 I. Title   II. Adamson, Olivia
 331.89′2822334′0941   HD5365.M6152.1984

 ISBN 0-905400-05-4

Cover photograph:
Orgreave 18 June 1984: John Harris IFL/Report
Design and artwork: Carol Brickley and Dale Evans
Typeset by Boldface Typesetters
Printed by A Wheaton & Co Ltd, Exeter and London

CONTENTS

ABBREVIATIONS

ACAS	Advisory Conciliation and Arbitration Service
ASLEF	Associated Society of Locomotive Engineers and Firemen
AUEW	Amalgamated Union of Engineering Workers
BACM	British Association of Colliery Management
BSC	British Steel Corporation
CBI	Confederation of British Industry
CEGB	Central Electricity Generating Board
CGT	Confédération Général de Travailleurs
CPGB	Communist Party of Great Britain
COSA	Colliery Overmen and Staff Association
DHSS	Department of Health and Social Security
EEC	European Economic Community
EEPTU	Electrical Electronic Telecommunications and Plumbing Union
EMA	Engineers and Managers Association
FRFI	*Fight Racism! Fight Imperialism!*
GMBATU	General Municipal Boilermakers and Allied Trades Union
IRA	Irish Republican Army
ISTC	Iron and Steel Trades Confederation
NACODS	National Association of Colliery Overseers Deputies and Shotfirers
NALGO	National and Local Government Officers Association
NCB	National Coal Board
NEC	National Executive Committee
NGA	National Graphical Association
NIO	Northern Ireland Office
NUM	National Union of Mineworkers
NUR	National Union of Railwaymen
POW	Prisoner of War
PSU	Police support unit
RCG	Revolutionary Communist Group
RCP	Revolutionary Communist Party
RUC	Royal Ulster Constabulary
STUC	Scottish Trades Union Congress
SWP	Socialist Workers Party
TGWU	Transport and General Workers Union
TUC	Trades Union Congress

TWELVE MONTHS OF STRUGGLE
A chronology of the strike

1983

1 September	Ian MacGregor takes over from Norman Siddall as NCB Chairman
21 October	Special NUM delegate conference votes for overtime ban against pit closures and 5.2% pay offer
31 October	Start of national overtime ban

1984

23 January	NCB says 19,000 sent home due to overtime ban. Many local disputes result
20 February	Scottish miners reject call for all-out strike over threatened closures in Scotland, but strike at Polmaise agreed
1 March	Closure of Cortonwood pit announced – with still five years to go. 55,000 Yorkshire miners called out on strike
6 March	Cut back of four million tonnes production announced by NCB
8 March	NUM Executive says Yorkshire and Scottish strikes official
12 March	Strike solid in Yorkshire, Kent and most of South Wales and Scotland
14 March	NCB obtains High Court injunction instructing Yorkshire NUM to call off pickets. Injunction ignored
15 March	David Jones, aged 24, killed at Ollerton while picketing. Notts area leaders call Notts miners out
18 March	Massive police operation starts: 3,000 police sent into Notts area, rising rapidly to 8,000 deployed at any one time. Kent miners on the way to Notts are turned back at roadblock at the Dartford tunnel
19 March	Notts miners say they will carry on working
20 March	Kent miners lose court case against police roadblocks
22 March	Power unions advise members to cross NUM picket lines
23 March	Police seal off entire county of Notts
26 March	NUM leaders tell TUC to stay out of strike. NACODS vote to accept pay offer
27 March	'Secret' caucus of right-wing NUM leaders issues call for national ballot, end of flying pickets and return to work
3 April	NUR tells members to block movements of coal

11 April	NACODS vote 7,638 to 6,661 in favour of strike – does not reach two-thirds majority needed
12 April	Kinnock calls for national ballot
19 April	NUM delegate conference in Sheffield votes against ballot. 10,000 miners rally outside in support
1 May	Notts miners given day off to demonstrate against strike outside Notts area HQ
2 May	Number of arrests is 1,479. Mass picket of Harworth Colliery is 10,000 strong
3 May	BSC starts bringing coal into steel plants with scab lorries
8 May	Coke supplies guaranteed by NUM for Llanwern
11 May	Coal trains into Ravenscraig start again after inter-union agreements
12 May	10,000 women march on Women Against Pit Closures demonstration in Barnsley
14 May	Mansfield rally of up to 40,000. Police attack in car park results in 56 riot charges and five of conspiracy
16 May	Anne Scargill arrested on picket line
17 May	Police siege of Blidworth, Notts
20 May	Len Murray declares one-day strikes in Yorks and Humberside and South Wales 'unconstitutional'
23 May	NUM leaders meet MacGregor for talks which collapse the same day
25 May	High Court instructs NUM not to discipline Notts miners. Coke convoys start from Orgreave coke depot to Scunthorpe steel works
26-28 May	Orgreave pickets build up
29 May	7,000 mass picket at Orgreave. 82 arrests, 69 injured
30 May	Arthur Scargill arrested at Orgreave. Massive mounted police charge. First barricade is lit
31 May	Orgreave battle continues
1 June	3,200 arrested so far during strike
6 June	Thatcher's involvement in averting rail strike revealed in leak to *Daily Mirror*
8 June	London miners' march and lobby of Parliament – 120 arrested. NUM and NCB meet for talks
13 June	Talks break down
15 June	Joe Green killed by a lorry whilst on picket duty at Ferrybridge power station
17 June	Police station attacked in Maltby, South Yorkshire
18 June	Mass picket at Orgreave. 6-7,000 pickets. 93 arrested, 59 injured. Scargill injured. Barricades built and set alight

27 June	Railway workers hold 24 hour strikes in London to support NUM. ISTC leaders say they will accept coal from anywhere
2 July	Notts area council elections – scabs take control
5-6 July	NUM and NCB meet for talks
9 July	National docks strike called over BSC use of scab labour at Immingham to unload iron ore. Police riot in Fitzwilliam, West Yorkshire
10 July	High Court grants order to Notts miners forbidding NUM conference to pass rule change allowing disciplining of working miners
11 July	Conference ignores ruling and passes rule changes
13 July	Arrests nearly 4,000 so far during strike
18 July	High Court grants Notts NUM application to have rule changes made null and void. Talks collapse over issue of 'uneconomic' pits
22 July	First national conference of Women Against Pit Closures
23 July	Dockers call off strike
28 July	NUM and TUC hold talks
31 July	South Wales area NUM fined £50,000 for contempt of court and assets seized
6 August	Two Yorks miners, Ken Foulstone and Robert Taylor, apply to High Court for ballot in Yorkshire
7 August	Surprise attacks by large numbers of pickets on NCB transport depot, Doncaster NCB HQ, Silverhill colliery and Harworth colliery, Notts
10 August	NUM special conference calls on TUC for support and passes rule changes on discipline for the second time
11 August	20,000 march on national Women Against Pit Closures demonstration in London
15 August	Welsh miners occupy Price Waterhouse offices in Birmingham
16 August	Sequestrators state they have seized £707,000 from South Wales NUM funds
20-24 August	Police battle for five days to get one scab into Easington colliery, Durham
21 August	TUC General Council hold first discussion of strike
22 August	Police attack in Armthorpe, Yorkshire
23 August	Second docks strike called over unloading of coal at Hunterston
30 August	South Wales miners seize transporter bridge in Newport and 80 miners occupy BSC jetty at Port Talbot
September	Throughout the month massive daily battles take place in Yorkshire and Kent to keep scabs out of pits

3 September	TUC conference starts – picket of 4-5,000 outside. TUC votes to support NUM. NCB-promoted 'back-to-work' day fails
9 September	Talks start and run through the week
15 September	Talks break down in London
19 September	Second docks strike ends
28 September	NACODS vote 82.5% in favour of strike. High Court rules Derbyshire strike 'unlawful' and Yorkshire strike 'unofficial'
30 September	Prior to start of Labour Party Conference Kinnock fails to stop motions criticising police actions in miners' strike
1 October	Arthur Scargill gets standing ovation at Labour Party conference. Arthur Scargill and four other NUM leaders served with High Court writ on floor of conference
2 October	Kinnock in speech at Conference 'abhors' 'all violence' 7,149 arrested, 39 gaoled so far during strike
3 October	NACODS and NCB go to ACAS
9 October	Tory Party Conference. Brittan guarantees government money for policing strike. Mass picket at Cortonwood
10 October	NUM fined £200,000 and Arthur Scargill fined £1,000 for contempt of court
11 October	New talks at ACAS
15 October	Talks fail – NCB insists on right to manage and close 'uneconomic' pits
Mid-October to mid-November	Daily battles take place between pickets and riot police in Yorkshire to prevent scabs going into pits
19 October	Power workers in EEPTU vote by 84% not to support miners
20 October	Michael Eaton appointed as NCB spokesperson instead of MacGregor
24 October	NACODS calls off strike after changes made by NCB to colliery review procedure. NUM rejects NCB's proposals
25 October	High Court orders NUM funds to be seized after NUM refuses to pay £200,000 contempt fine
28 October	*Sunday Times* carries story that NUM official has visited Libya
29 October	NCB removes Eaton as spokesperson
31 October	7,428 arrests, 49 imprisoned so far during strike
3 November	Kinnock announces that he is 'too busy' to attend major NUM rallies. High Court grants injunction to North Derbyshire scabs forbidding area NUM to spend any more money on the strike.

Price Waterhouse seizes NUM assets.
Special delegate conference affirms continuation of strike

6 November	3,000 attend NUM mass rally in Edinburgh
8 November	6,000 attend NUM mass rally in Sheffield
9 November	Mass picket at Cortonwood to stop one scab
12 November	Petrol bombs and barricades in Yorkshire. Pickets battle with police in South Wales. Thatcher compares pickets to IRA bombers
13 November	Willis attacks 'the brick, the bolt and the petrol bomb' at South Wales miners' rally – noose is lowered in front of him
21 November	Government announces further £1 to be deducted from DHSS benefits paid to striking miners' families, on top of non-existent £15 strike pay already deducted
24 November	NCB claims 5,952 go back in one week. After this, number falls off rapidly
1 December	Herbert Brewer appointed as receiver in control of NUM funds. 8,731 arrested, 87 gaoled and 17 sent to detention centres so far during strike
3 December	NUM delegate conference supports decision to defy courts
4 December	Brewer fails to get hold of NUM funds in Luxemburg
7 December	Brewer resigns, Michael Arnold takes over. TUC says will not take illegal action in support of miners
20 December	Notts Area Council vote to change rules and loosen ties with national NUM

1985

1 January	Arrests stand at 9,145 in England and Wales, 1,406 in Scotland (up to 7 December 1984). Terry French and Chris Tazey, Kent miners, sentenced to five years and three years respectively
17 January	One day rail strike in Yorkshire and East Midlands region in support of railway workers sacked at Coalville depot
24 January	NUM EC agrees to meet NCB following meeting between Smith and Heathfield
29 January	Preliminary talks break down
15 February	Eight point surrender document issued by NCB after secret meetings with Willis. NUM and NACODS reject document. Arrests stand at 9,542 in England and Wales, 1,471 in Scotland (up to 1 February 1985) so far during strike
19 February	TUC meets Thatcher and later Walker, and produces final document
20 February	NUM EC rejects 'TUC document'.

21 February	Special delegate conference rejects 'TUC document'
24 February	Major demonstration in London in support of miners. 101 arrests as police attack march
25 February	NCB claim highest Monday back-to-work figure since start of strike – 3,807
1 March	Durham, Lancashire, South Wales and COSA vote for return without an agreement. Scotland adds rider that return conditional on amnesty for the more than 700 sacked miners
2 March	Yorkshire votes by four votes to continue strike
3 March	Special delegate conference at TUC HQ votes 98-91 for a return on 5 March
4 March	Scotland delegate conference votes 7-6 to stay out. Yorkshire votes to go back. Kent votes to stay out
5 March	Miners in Yorkshire and South Wales return to work behind banners. Miners at some Yorkshire and South Wales pits turn back at picket lines mounted by Kent miners. Half Yorkshire miners still out, half Scottish miners and all Kent miners. Scottish miners delegates vote 10-5 for return
6 March	10,000 still on strike in Yorkshire, Scotland and Kent
8 March	Kinnock visits Scottish Labour Party Conference
10/11 March	Kent and Scotland vote to return to work

POLICING THE MINERS' STRIKE

Policing

The Chief Constable of Notts estimated 164,508 pickets were turned away from Notts during the first 27 weeks of the strike, ie more than 6,000 per week. (*Financial Times* 4 March 1985)

In South Yorkshire 50 police stations were damaged during the strike (*Financial Times* 4 March 1985)

551 complaints have been made against the police during the strike, more than half of them involving assault. (*The Guardian* 9 March 1985)

During the strike there were 1.5 million deployments of police from 43 forces. 8,100 were deployed in one week at the high point during Orgreave. (*Financial Times* 4 March 1985)

Arrests and charges

By the end of February 9,750 had been arrested, 10,335 charges had been made and 7,874 charged, according to the Home Office. 5,528 cases had been dealt with, resulting in 4,112 convictions and 1,416 acquittals. (*The Guardian* 4 March 1985). In Scotland, 1,471 had been arrested up to 1 February. (*New Stateman*).

152 have been given gaol sentences with 61 others receiving sentences involving custody either before or after the trial. (*The Guardian* 4 March 1985). Many more miners were, and some still are, held on remand.

Major charges

Section 5 of the Public Order Act – Conduct likely to cause a breach of the peace	4089
Obstruction of police	1682
Obstruction of Highway	640
Criminal damage	1015
Arson	15
Assault on police	359
Assault occasioning Actual Bodily Harm	424
Conspiracy and Protection of Property Act 1875	275
Unlawful assembly	509
Affray	21
Riot	137
Threats to kill	5
Murder	3

Victimisations

By 11 March 1985 766 miners have been sacked by the NCB for 'offences' allegedly committed in the strike. (*Financial Times* 12 March 1985)

INTRODUCTION

The fight goes on

The most heroic strike that the British working class has seen for decades ended on 5 March 1985. The year long miners' strike, the longest major industrial battle in British history, has changed the political consciousness of hundreds of thousands of people. The courage and determination of the striking miners, their families and communities will have a lasting impact on the working class struggle in Britain in the years ahead.

The strike may have ended but, in the words of Arthur Scargill, President of the National Union of Mineworkers (NUM) 'the dispute goes on'. At a press conference on 3 March, soon after the union's national delegate conference had voted narrowly, 98-91, to return to work without an agreement, Arthur Scargill said:

> '. . . we will continue to fight pit closures and job losses – and make no mistake, don't underestimate this union's ability to fight pit closures and job losses.
>
> 'This union will continue to fight, and if that means we have to consider taking action again then we shall do so . . . '

Scargill made clear that the major reason for the return to work was the fact:

Scargill attacks TUC betrayal

> '. . . that the trade union movement in Britain, with a few notable exceptions have left this union isolated. They have not carried out TUC congress decisions, to their eternal shame.
>
> 'We faced not an employer but a Government aided and abetted by the judiciary, the police and you people in the media. At the end of this time our people have suffered tremendous hardship . . . '

Scargill himself vehemently opposed calling off the strike. The NUM National Executive however was split 11-11 and did not recommend a course of action to the delegate conference. But faced with many more miners being forced back to work by hunger, deprivation and debt, the delegates narrowly voted for an organised return to work without an agreement. The pressures which had built up against areas which wanted to continue the strike had proved too great.

It took another week before the Kent miners, and sections of Scottish and Yorkshire miners went back. Many had been determined to stay out until those miners victimised during the strike had been given their jobs back. In the end they were forced to accept the inevitable –

1

the vast majority of miners had gone back and would fight for rein-statement by other means. But the 'dispute goes on'.

NCB on the offensive Many clashes with a National Coal Board (NCB) management, determined to drive home its present advantage, have taken place and will continue to take place. Union officials are finding their union work is restricted, that they are being consulted little, if at all, on shift patterns and that previous 'custom and practice' agreements have been dropped. Clashes between miners and scabs are widespread and many more miners are being sacked or sent home in a number of areas. While some miners have been reinstated others are being sacked as more cases go through the courts. By 11 March, of the 766 miners who had been sacked nationally, 111 had been reinstated. The Scotland Area Direc-tor, Mr Wheeler, was still refusing to take anyone back. The fight by the NUM to regain the initiative will be a long one – taking into account the continuing disputes and growing splits within the NUM itself. On 14 March three areas, Nottinghamshire, Leicestershire and South Derbyshire, agreed to challenge the authority of the NUM Exe-cutive on the continuing overtime ban (Notts had lifted it two weeks earlier) and on the proposed ballot for a 50p levy on all miners to help those striking miners victimised as a result of the strike. There is growing pressure also to accept the NCB pay offer of 5.2 per cent – outstanding for the past two years – which is conditional on lifting the overtime ban and resuming 'normal working'. The dispute will cer-tainly go on and it looks like being bitter and long drawn out.

The miners' strike began as a struggle of the miners and their com-munities to defend their jobs – to halt pit closures. It inevitably became something much more fundamental because of the political and eco-nomic context in which it was taking place.

In the RCG Manifesto, *The revolutionary road to communism in Britain*, written some six months before the miners' strike began we said:

> 'The growing economic crisis of British imperialism threatens the alliance that has tied the organised working class to the capitalist system in Britain. The attack on living standards, the growing unemployment and poverty is eroding the material conditions that have consolidated the political hold the labour aristocracy has over the whole working class. This process, while still in its early stages, has nevertheless led to a developing crisis within the Labour Party and trade union movement. This in turn has had its impact on the more radical elements of the new middle class and therefore among the British socialist organisations which draw their membership from such groups. Finally the more oppressed sections of the work-ing class are increasingly demonstrating their independence from the traditional organisations of the working class. The split in the British working class is inevitably growing . . . ' (page 117)

This approach made us very clear right from the start about develop-ments in the miners' strike.

The split in the NUM For the miners' strike to take place at all a split was necessary in the NUM, primarily between two distinct sections of miners. The one

2

higher paid with relatively secure employment working in high investment, high productivity pits – especially in the Notts area. The other lower paid and/or under constant threat of redundancies, working in less productive pits. Creating such divisions in the NUM has been a conscious strategy of the NCB since 1974. It was a Labour government which introduced productivity deals and which allowed miners in high productivity, high investment pits to earn considerably more than their fellow workers in less productive pits.

The second factor which lies behind the strike is that the government picked the time and place of the dispute and from the beginning it was determined to destroy the NUM under Arthur Scargill's leadership. It was relying on the deep divisions in the NUM to prevent any serious resistance to pit closures. And it was confident, having recently crushed the National Graphical Association (NGA), that the Trades Union Congress (TUC) would have no stomach for any real fight.

The strike went so far because, from the beginning, the striking miners and their leaders refused to allow their struggle to be limited by the narrow self-interest of better off layers of the working class, either in their own ranks or their organisations and political parties.

So the less privileged miners – those with most to lose – dictated the terms of the strike. The better paid and more secure miners (eg Notts) and the 'moderate' trade union leaders were prevented from

Thatcher's strategy

Photo:
Monktonhall
colliery, East
Lothian, march
back to work, 7
March 1985
Rick Matthews/
IFL

3

imposing their will on the strike in spite of support from the Thatcher government, NCB and Labour Party. This was the significance of the refusal to hold a national ballot.

The split in the NUM was a fundamental feature of the strike. It was a split that was mirrored throughout the Labour and trade union movement as the strike progressed and workers were inevitably forced to take sides. It says a great deal for the courage and determination of the striking miners and their communities that it took twelve months of bitter struggle, with very little support from the organised trade union movement, before the Labour and trade union leaders were able decisively to undermine the strike.

State against the miners

Once it became clear early on in the strike that the opportunist forces – what the media likes to call the 'moderates' – within the NUM and outside of it in the Labour Party and trade union movement were unable to significantly restrict the progress of the strike, the full force of the state was used against the striking miners. A national co-ordinated police action was directed against them involving 20,000 police with some 8,000 operational at any one time. This action was coordinated by Scotland Yard using massive computer-backed data gathering for intelligence. Road blocks, political questioning, beatings, illegal fingerprinting and photographing, snatch squads, phone taps, infiltrators and *agents provocateurs,* were all used against the striking miners. And miners on picket lines were brutalised and attacked by baton-wielding police in full riot gear.

Alongside the police violence was the mobilisation of the courts and the law against the striking miners. General Sir Frank Kitson explained this process in his book *Low intensity operations, subversion, insurgency and peace-keeping.* Kitson said that the law is:

'just another weapon in the government's arsenal and it becomes little more than a propaganda cover for the disposal of unwanted members of the public.'

Kitson's views draw together years of experience of British strategy in counter-revolutionary violence against liberation movements throughout the world and, of course, in the Six Counties of Ireland from 1970-1972. This strategy was used during the miners' strike particularly in the arrest of leading NUM militants and in the use of political bail conditions explicitly barring striking miners from picketing or approaching NCB property, or both – that is, the law was being used to remove 'unwanted members' of the NUM from the picket lines. The right to picket, to protest effectively became a 'criminal offence'. Miners fighting for their jobs were 'criminalised' during the strike.

While using its 'laws' to attack the striking miners, the state used every means at its disposal to sustain the scab miners and their organisations – police protection and private business finance – offering bribes and other inducements to persuade miners to come back to work. And all this was accompanied by a propaganda barrage from the press and TV, which, day by day as the miners' strike progressed, became little more than a mouthpiece for the government and the NCB.

4

Faced with state repression the miners responded on the same lines as the oppressed have responded everywhere. The lessons of Ireland, of Brixton and Liverpool 8 were very quickly learned under such conditions. The miners built barricades, set them alight, overturned cars, hurled bricks and stakes in self-defence against the police. They were forced to go way beyond the legal, constitutional and peaceful methods of struggle so beloved by opportunists like Kinnock, Murray, Bill Sirs and others.

Miners fight back

James Anderton, Chief Constable of Manchester, blurted out at an early stage the ruling class approach to this, when he said mass pickets were:

'acts of terrorism without the bullet and the bomb . . . '

The use of the term 'terrorist' is no coincidence or mistake. Any force which threatens the power of the ruling class is invariably labelled 'terrorist' – it was part of an ideological offensive to isolate the striking miners from other workers, as dangerous 'extremists'. And, in particular, it was very important for the ruling class to try to isolate Arthur Scargill, the one major trade union leader who stood by his class.

No one more than Arthur Scargill embodies the shift that has taken place in working class politics as a result of the miners' strike. He made it clear that he would rather go to prison than betray his class. His refusal to condemn miners' 'violence' in defence of their jobs and communities showed him again standing by his class. When he did this he necessarily came into conflict not only with the ruling class and its courts but also with opportunists like Kinnock, Willis, Sirs and the rest. While Thatcher stood by her class, Scargill stood by his.

The miners' strike was a political threat to the traditional Labour and trade union leadership. The opportunists, the staunch upholders of the old order, were terrified that their carefully built institutions, based on years of treacherous compromise with the ruling class, would be blown apart if the miners' strike continued outside their control. For this reason, throughout the strike, the Labour Party and TUC leadership did everything in their power to dissociate themselves from the militant leadership of the NUM.

Kinnock against miners

Kinnock supported a national ballot and condemned the 'violence' of the miners' picket lines under the guise of 'condemning all violence . . . without fear or favour'. By sitting on the fence, he betrayed the miners. Willis did likewise, as did most trade union leaders. Both Kinnock and Willis used the NUM/Libyan 'connection' to undermine the NUM leadership while remaining silent over the seizure of NUM funds by ruling class courts at the end of October. Kinnock refused to speak at five NUM rallies organised at a crucial point in the strike in early November and so it goes on. On the central issues of workers' democracy versus ruling class democracy, workers' violence versus ruling class violence and 'illegality' versus legality Kinnock and Willis sided with the ruling class.

With 'friends' like these who needed enemies? Lenin's characterisation of the opportunists as the 'principal enemy', as 'better defenders of the bourgeoisie than the bourgeoisie itself' was demonstrated time and again during the miners' strike. 'Without their leadership of the workers, the bourgeoisie could not remain in power'. Without their leadership of the workers, Thatcher and the NCB could not have driven the miners back to work.

Their lack of solidarity with the miners' strike must be contrasted with their solidarity with each other. When Willis was rightly jeered and booed at a South Wales miners' rally in November for his role in undermining the miners' strike, and a noose was lowered from the balcony above his head, almost every trade union leader came to his defence and attacked the miners for treating him in that way.

Scargill and Larkin

A parallel has been drawn between James Larkin, the revolutionary leader of the Irish Transport and General Workers Union (ITGWU) at the time of the Dublin lock-out in 1913 and Arthur Scargill – between Larkinism and Scargillism. In 1913, the poorest and most oppressed Dublin workers organised in the ITGWU led by James Larkin and James Connolly, had to confront the reactionary alliance of the Dublin capitalists, the British imperialist ruling class and the leaders of the British Labour and trade union movement.

The Dublin workers fought a courageous and determined eight month struggle in the course of which they created their own workers' defence force against police violence – the Irish Citizen Army. The one thing they needed to ensure victory was real solidarity action from the working class in Britain. Rank and file workers in transport unions and indeed the South Wales miners did respond by organising sympathetic strike action and making donations. The Dublin workers attracted support from revolutionary nationalists in Ireland, socialist leaders like John Maclean in Scotland, militant suffragettes like Sylvia Pankhurst and many thousands of rank and file workers.

However the British Labour and trade union leaders moved into action immediately to stamp out solidarity action. Larkin was forced to appeal to British workers directly and urged them to reject their leaders who he described as 'serpents'. Unfortunately, the strength of the opportunist trade unionist leadership proved too great. Ben Tillett, previously regarded as a militant leader and who had stood on platforms with Larkin calling for the arming of workers, led the attack on Larkin at the special TUC congress in December 1913. Tillett turned against Larkin because Larkin and the struggle he represented threatened to undermine the control of the opportunist leaders over the British working class, that is, to split the British labour movement. The British Labour and trade union leaders were as terrified of Larkinism as the Dublin employers. William Martin Murphy, leader of the Dublin employers, made clear what was so terrifying about Larkinism. He said:

"It is not a question of an attack on trade unionism at all. I have been in business for nearly 50 years and I have never before known anything like Larkinism. It is not trade unionism in the ordinary sense at all.'

In just the same way today, the government, the media, the Labour

6

Party and trade union leaders continually denounce what they call Scargillism. The parallel is an obvious one – 'it is not trade unionism in the ordinary sense at all'. The struggle of oppressed workers not only threatens the ruling class but also those Labour and trade union leaders who have hung on to their powerful positions in the labour movement through negotiations, compromise and compliance with the ruling class, its laws and institutions. In just the same way during the miners' strike, the justifiable attack on Willis for undermining the strike brought unity in the ranks of the trade union leaders against Scargill and against the striking miners.

The crisis of imperialism will inevitably lead to the disintegration of the Labour Party, as the social base of the labour aristocracy shrinks and its ability to control the working class movement is undermined. The miners' strike demonstrated that this development is inevitable.

Photo: Rossington—Women's Action Group march on 4 March 1985 John Harris/IFL

7

Perhaps the most politically decisive factor in the miners' strike has been the fact that, as the strike progressed, the most politically conscious miners and their supporters have recognised the need to ally themselves with the oppressed fighting British imperialism at home or abroad. That is miners are starting to argue for an anti-imperialist standpoint in the British labour movement.

Very quickly the miners drew connections between their treatment and that of black workers in South Africa, the treatment of the Irish people in the Six Counties and that of black youth by the racist British police here at home. This was expressed dramatically in the headline of *The Miner* in July 1984 'Belfast comes to Blidworth'. More recently Kate Whiteside, a member of the new national co-ordinating committee of the NUM Women's Action Group, relating her growing political involvement during the strike said:

> 'Police (were) treating people rough: coming in at six in the morning, and frightening the children. Suddenly I said "my God, that's been happening to blacks for years".' (*The Guardian* 19 February 1985)

It has been because miners have recognised that a defeat for their struggle would force thousands of them into unemployment and poverty that they have fought in such a determined and courageous way. Recognising what awaits them should they be defeated, they have, through the practical experience gained in a determined struggle against the British state, begun to see where their real interests lie and who are their real allies.

A victory in an outright sense for the miners, of the 1972/74 Saltley Gate kind, appeared unlikely throughout the strike because of the bitter split in the NUM and the growing split in the organised trade union movement. After the TUC Conference in September such a victory became virtually impossible. It became clear that the split in the organised working class movement is not simply one between the trade union 'bureaucracy' and the rank and file but goes down deeper into the ranks of the working class. Key workers, dockers, power and steel workers, lorry drivers and sections of miners themselves – on the whole the better paid in more secure jobs – were scabbing on the miners' strike.

However, as many miners have pointed out, and Arthur Scargill has stated on numerous occasions, the year-long struggle itself represented a political victory. The lessons learned, the forms of struggle adopted, and the new organisations thrown up during the strike will have a lasting impact on the working class movement in this country. At a rally in Trafalgar Square just over a week before the end of the strike, Arthur Scargill drove home the essential points:

> 'The strike has brought a new dimension to British politics with hundreds of thousands of people involved in support groups not only in this country, but all over the world . . .
>
> 'We have already achieved a magnificent victory by showing that working people are not prepared to lie down under this Thatcher government. Stand firm. Lift your hearts and eyes to a new

horizon and towards saving this industry and our jobs . . . '

The miners' strike has transformed political life for hundreds of thousands of people, in particular for the striking miners and their families and for thousands upon thousands of their supporters. The political gains of the strike are very significant ones and if built on will lead to a lasting advance for the British working class movement. What are these gains?

Lessons of the strike

First, the mining communities and hundreds of thousands of their supporters have come to understand the vicious class character of the British imperialist state as they have experienced its police, courts and prisons. Many now recognise the need for disciplined organisation to defend themselves against it.

Second, thousands of workers have come to know the character of the leadership of the Labour Party and trade union movement and realise that a new fighting movement can only be built after a decisive break with these leaders and the section of the working class which follows them.

Third, the mining communities, themselves forced to fight with the brick, the barricade and the petrol bomb against Thatcher's national riot police, have come for the first time to see allies in those fighting for freedom in the Six Counties of Ireland and in black people forced to fight against the racist police state in Britain.

Fourth, perhaps the most important political development in the strike has been the critical and often leading role of the women in the mining communities in defending and sustaining the strike through organisation, demonstrations, street activities and defence of their relatives and friends in prison for supporting the strike.

Women's support groups—major gain of strike

The women's support groups in the mining areas and miners' support groups in the towns and cities are a major gain of the strike. Their work is still crucial to continue the struggle against victimisation of striking miners and to defend the imprisoned miners. Increased activity from these groups now the strike has ended will mean solid organisation and experience exists to defend miners and other workers in the future.

At a Chesterfield rally in commemoration of International Women's Day on 9 March 1985, Scargill acknowledged these important points when he urged the women's support groups to rededicate themselves to the struggle even though the strike had ended.

'This is not the end. It's the beginning because you are part of this union and must remain part of the miners' union . . .

'We've got to take this fight forward and step up the campaign. The women's support groups have got to take on a broader role.

'You must become involved in the wider issues. Learn and understand that rate-capping affects each and every one of us and that the peace movement is absolutely important . . . '

Scargill went on to demand of the Labour and trade union leaders that they stop equivocating on the demand for an amnesty for all miners victimised during the strike. He made it clear he was referring to all miners when he said:

9

Political prisoners

'Those men who have been arrested and gaoled as far as I'm concerned are political prisoners. They've been gaoled because they fought for this union . . . '

Scargill demanded that any future Labour government 'wipe clean' the stain against all those arrested.

Finally he launched a bitter attack on the union leaders, particularly those in the power industry, who he said:

' . . . should hang their heads in eternal shame for what they have done during this dispute.

'They can come forward with whatever arguments they wish but they will never be able to erase the fact that when the chips were down they supported Margaret Thatcher and turned their backs on the NUM'. (*Newsline*, 11 March 1985)

Scargill's speeches continually pose a way forward for the working class which goes beyond the traditional methods of struggle of the trade union movement. It would indeed be progress if the working class women who have been involved in the support groups took their experience into the movements for peace, against rate-capping, took a stand in solidarity with those fighting racism, and with those fighting imperialism in Ireland, South Africa and throughout the world.

To become 'involved in the wider issues' they will have to fight many Labour Party and Communist Party members within the NUM and outside in the wider trade union movement for the right to exist and develop their work. For there are those who will not follow the path of these new class organisations and are intent on reasserting the deadly grip of traditional labour movement methods of organisation, negotiation and compromise.

The British left and miners

The major organisations to the left of the Labour Party have without exception ignored the split in the working class which has deepened throughout the strike. In the case of the Communist Party of Great Britain (CPGB) they have attempted at every stage to cover up for it. The dangers of this are already becoming clear. The *Morning Star* reported on 9 March that:

'Scottish miners' leaders yesterday were greatly encouraged by positive support from Labour leader Neil Kinnock in their campaign to get hundreds of sacked miners their jobs back.'

Kinnock has, in fact, refused to support an amnesty for *all* miners sacked. The Vice-President of the NUM, Mick McGahey, a leading member of the CPGB, has already met Kinnock and an invitation has been extended to Kinnock and Willis to take part in the Scottish Miners Gala later this year. The crucial lessons of the year-long strike are being thrown aside as some NUM leaders and officials are all too ready to build bridges with the opportunists who did so much damage to their strike.

Real communists oppose any attempt at reconciliation with such opportunists. Those advocating 'unity' with such forces are, as Lenin argued, 'objectively defending the *enslavement* of the workers by the imperialist bourgeoisie with the aid of its best agents in the labour

10

movement'. Communists and socialists have to abandon their pre-occupation with the privileged minority of the working class and their leaders, and go down *'lower* and *deeper* to the real masses'. That Lenin said is the 'whole meaning and whole purport of the struggle against opportunism.'

The miners' strike has not only confirmed this by exposing the role of the organised trade union movement during the strike, but also because a year of bitter struggle has thrown up new class organisations of the kind that would be capable of taking the struggle of the working class forward. The work of women's support groups and the miners' support groups made a crucial contribution to the strike precisely because they were outside the control of Labour and trade union bureaucracies. If these support groups continue to carry out the work necessary to defend miners victimised and imprisoned during the strike, and take their experience into other working class struggles then indeed the miners' strike 1984-5 will have 'brought a new dimension to British politics'.

Throughout the strike the Revolutionary Communist Group has fully backed the striking miners under the leadership of Arthur Scargill. Our members have organised material and financial support to the strikers, joined and worked in miners' support groups, and been on picket lines. Our paper *Fight Racism! Fight Imperialism!* has made the miners' strike the central political feature of each issue as the strike has developed. We have learned from the strike and drawn political lessons from it.

The chapters of this book appeared as articles in *Fight Racism! Fight Imperialism!* They have been reprinted with minor alterations and additions and reflect the RCG's political assessment of the strike as the events took place. Towards the end of the strike in January the RCG argued for a new emphasis of political work to break the impasse of the strike at that time. Chapter 8 of this book 'Go out to the people' argues for this new emphasis – for an attempt to organise the thousands of ordinary people outside the organised labour movement who wanted the miners to win and see Thatcher defeated.

Chapters 1 and 2 were written by Olivia Adamson, Terry Marlowe and David Reed; chapters 3, 4 and 5 by Olivia Adamson, David Reed and Maxine Williams; and chapters 6, 7, 8, 9 and 10 by Olivia Adamson and David Reed. The other articles in the book were printed in *Fight Racism! Fight Imperialism!* and all give further insight into developments during the strike and our political work at the time. Soon after the strike ended we received an article from Laurence McKeown, an Irish political prisoner in the H-Blocks of Long Kesh, expressing his and other political prisoners' solidarity with the strike. We are privileged to print this article as part of the book.

Finally, the book would not have been possible except for the hard, sustained political work of RCG comrades and supporters during the miners' strike.

David Reed
15 March 1985

11

MINERS ON STRIKE

People versus State

After two weeks of bitter struggle the miners' fight to save jobs dramatically demonstrated the fundamental political features of working class struggle in this period. These are first and foremost the split in the working class movement. Second the reactionary and oppressive character of the British imperialist state, its police, laws and courts. Third, the ruthlessness with which the British ruling class in a period of intense crisis will use all means at its disposal to crush any opposition to its rule. And finally that only by going beyond legal, constitutional and traditional methods of trade union struggle can such a fight be won.

On 1 March 1984 Ian MacGregor, chairman of the National Coal Board (NCB) and previously architect of the destruction of the British steel industry, gave four weeks notice of the closure of Cortonwood colliery in Yorkshire. The pit has at least five years working life left. The Tory government, encouraged by its victory against the National Graphical Association (NGA), had decided that the moment had come to take on the miners. Given the level of coal stocks and with warmer weather on the way, Thatcher and Co knew that this was the best moment to test the ability of the National Union of Mineworkers (NUM) to defend jobs, given that any strike would have to be a long one. On 6 March MacGregor announced NCB plans for 1984/5 involving a 4 million tonne cut in production, 20 pit closures and 20,000 redundancies. Arthur Scargill, President of the NUM, argued that this plan would actually mean 40 pit closures and 40,000 redundancies and that the NCB's eventual aim was to reduce the coal industry from 174 to 100 pits and the workforce from 184,000 to 100,000. Two days later in a blatant attempt to bribe miners into accepting redundancies, the NCB announced a massive increase in redundancy payments. The payment for a miner with 30 years service trebled from £11,197 to £33,262. It was now clear that the long running overtime ban was not going to prevent pit closures. The time for a decisive battle had come.

The government was relying on deep divisions which exist in the NUM to prevent any serious resistance to pit closures. These divisions are a reflection of the split in the working class movement as a whole. This split, between the relatively privileged upper layers of the working class and the ever growing numbers of workers condemned to unemployment and poverty as the crisis deepens, is the central political feature of our time. It is precisely because the official Labour and

MacGregor announces production cutbacks

trade union movement represents the interests *only* of the privileged upper layers that it has not merely failed to defend workers' interests, but also actively sabotaged serious struggles. This has been seen time and again, most strikingly in the health workers' dispute in 1982 and the NGA dispute at the end of 1983. The difference this time, in the latest miners' dispute, is that a section of trade unionists under threat have, so far, determinedly refused to allow their struggle to be defeated by a privileged layer of workers within their own ranks.

Productivity deals

The creation of the divisions in the NUM has been a conscious strategy of the ruling class since 1974. In 1977 it was the Labour government that began the process with a productivity deal which meant that miners in high productivity, high investment pits could earn considerably more than their fellow workers in less productive pits. Today a miner in Nottingham can earn more in bonus payments alone – around £80 per week – than the basic take home pay of a surface worker elsewhere – just under £74. By these means two distinct sections of miners are being created: one higher paid with relatively secure employment working in high investment, high productivity pits; the other low paid, now under constant threat of redundancies, and working in less productive pits. Arthur Scargill has argued that some of these latter pits have been deliberately starved of necessary investment. From 1972 to 1984 over 100,000 miners' jobs have disappeared and 115 pits have been closed down. MacGregor's strategy is simple and ruthless: to pour money into the productive pits and to buy off the miners at those pits through separate productivity bonuses for each pit – and thus divide the NUM even further.

Strike begins 12 March 1984

Up to now this NCB strategy has been successful. Twice since Arthur Scargill became President of the NUM he has failed to secure the necessary 55 per cent majority in national ballots to call a national strike against pit closures. Isolated sections of the NUM have been left to fight alone as happened with Kinneil colliery in Scotland in 1982/3 and Ty-Mawr Merthyr, South Wales, in February 1983. Faced with the stark reality of MacGregor's latest announced plan which Arthur Scargill had correctly foreseen, thousands of miners had no choice but to fight. This time no national ballot was called. Instead the NUM Executive called on local areas to take strike action from Monday 12 March following large pickets of the NUM headquarters in Sheffield.

On Monday 12 March, the whole of Yorkshire and Kent, and most of South Wales and Scotland were out. Heavy picketing ensured 100 per cent support in those areas by the following weekend. Early reluctance in Scotland and Wales was due to the fact that Yorkshire had not supported them in previous calls to action. The NCB meanwhile took court action against the Yorkshire NUM and obtained an injunction against illegal picketing. This was ignored and mass picketing continued particularly in Nottinghamshire where miners are traditionally moderate and are relatively secure with highly productive seams. The NCB has so far not gone back to court. Clashes occurred between police, miners and pickets. During one running battle at Ollerton, a young miner, David Jones from South Kirby in Yorkshire, was killed as police and scabs attacked NUM pickets. The consequence of not

David Jones killed 15 March 1984

14

holding a national ballot has been that the tactics of the struggle have been dictated by the miners under threat and not by the more privileged sections of the union. This is the political significance of the mass pickets aimed at forcing the more privileged miners to join the strike. Those who are now calling for a national ballot are, in effect, demanding that the more privileged sections of the NUM be allowed yet another opportunity to impose their own narrow interests on all miners. This is why the ruling class and its media are backing this call. It soon became very obvious to Thatcher and MacGregor that the miners were not going to be stopped either by the dictates of the more privileged sections of the union or by court action and piecemeal policing. So the organised power of the state was brought to bear in a police operation designed to physically crush the miners' struggle.

MASSIVE POLICE OPERATION

On Sunday 18 March, in a huge operation, 3,000 police reinforcements were sent into the Nottinghamshire area, equipped with riot gear, with some of them being put up in army camps. TV viewers were treated to the sight of the police operations room at Scotland Yard where movements of police (data on their equipment, their training in riots, use of dogs etc), pickets' movements, local intelligence, car numbers, ballot predictions and breakdowns, and without doubt telephone conversa-

Photo: Arrest on the picket line

15

tions, were all collated. This system was last used in the 1981 uprisings and has been refined since then. In addition, Kent miners going North to picket were stopped at the Dartford Tunnel and threatened with arrest if they left the county. (They turned round and went another way.) Police also began to stop and turn back Yorkshire miners on their way to the Nottingham pits – but thousands still got through to picket every working pit. Many pickets hid out overnight in Sherwood Forest and were guided through the back ways by sympathetic Nottingham miners. The number of pits closed rose from 127 on Monday 19 March to 146 on Wednesday 21 March. On Thursday, police tried to seal off every pit in a ring of half a mile radius. Every car was stopped and searched. They smashed in one car's windscreen with a crowbar.

At the Yorkshire NUM headquarters in Barnsley, 1,000 miners gathered to defend their union from bailiffs in the event of the NCB's court action being successful. An arrest led to attempts to turn over a police van whereupon the man was released. Reinforcements of police rushed in and in the ensuing fighting the press was justly attacked by the miners. MacGregor prudently called off his court action. By Friday 23 March the police had been forced to seal off the entire county of Nottinghamshire. Miners were arrested if they did not turn back at road blocks. Pickets that did get through – up to 1,000 per day – were kept from working miners by massed ranks of police. In the same week, some train drivers and seamen refused to move coal and the open cast miners in the Transport and General Workers Union (TGWU) also refused to move any coal.

In the third full week of the strike, pickets found new ways of voicing their anger. For two days running on 27 and 28 March, 700 miners tried to prevent the 1,000 workers at the NCB headquarters in Doncaster from getting in to work. Masses of police were drafted in to keep the headquarters open. Stones were thrown by pickets at police, several of whom were injured. Miners have also, in 150 strong convoys, blocked up all the lanes of the A1 and M1 motorways by driving at 12mph. Coachloads of police were used to force miners off the roads. A convoy on the A38 in South Derbyshire on 28 March resulted in 48 arrests, with police smashing car windows. In return police were injured by being dragged along by cars and police coaches were smashed up. An estimated 20,000 police are involved in this national operation to defeat the miners' strike. At any one time up to 8,000 police are involved in violently preventing miners forming mass pickets. This police operation is costing *£500,000 a day*. The ruling class is never short of money to police its own interests. In spite of all this between 130-140 pits remain closed – the rest can only be kept open by police violence.

UNITY—BUT WHAT KIND OF UNITY?

The miners' dispute is not a simple trade union struggle or a simple fight for jobs. It has become a fight against the growing and inevitable repression directed by a ruling class which will use any means necessary to protect its wealth and privileges. It has exposed once again the alliance of forces ranged against the working class: the ruling class, its laws, courts and police, and its agents in the working class movement. The miners can only win this struggle by refusing to allow their fight to be limited by the legal and constitutional rules laid down by the Thatcher government or by the narrow self-interest of privileged layers of the working class, their organisations and political parties. Any determined struggle will inevitably bring them into confrontation with the representatives of these privileged layers both within the NUM and outside it.

Right-wing leaders demand ballot

On Tuesday 27 March nine members of the NUM Executive held a 'secret' caucus from which they issued a very public call for a national ballot and a return to work. These leaders, like Syd Vincent (Lancashire), Ray Chadburn (Notts) and Jack Jones (Leicestershire) are prepared to sacrifice thousands of miners' jobs in order to maintain the privileged position of the miners they represent. They are devotees of the Len Murray school – the luxury-carpeted offices, lunches with the management, lie down and submit style of trade unionism. They are agents of the ruling class in the working class movement. Unity with such people would be the unity of the graveyard for the mass of miners. A few days after this meeting the Lancashire miners, deeply divided, voted to go back to work.

To win any miners' strike depends on solidarity action from other workers particularly those involved with the movement or use of coal. Two railway unions, National Union of Railwaymen (NUR) and the Associated Society of Locomotive Engineers and Firemen (ASLEF), the National Union of Seamen, the TGWU and the Iron and Steel Trades Confederation (ISTC) have pledged support. But again there are the same inevitable splits in their ranks. Within a day of pledging support to the miners' strike Bill Sirs (ISTC) declared on Friday 30 March:

Bill Sirs scabs

'We want to support as much as we can but I am not here to see the steel industry crucified on someone else's altar.'

What Bill Sirs means is that he will not allow *his* privileges and *his* position to be threatened in a fight for basic working class rights. This, it should be remembered, was the man who in 1981 wanted to go to South Africa in order to pull black workers 'out of the dark ages and provide the sort of training shop stewards have here', and who opposed mandatory sanctions against South Africa on the grounds it would undermine British jobs. Once again this racism shows that he is not prepared to allow his privileged position to be threatened by the revolutionary struggle of black workers in South Africa against imperialist oppression and exploitation. Unity with the likes of Sirs would be the unity of defeat. Workers in other unions who want to unite and fight with the miners will be forced to confront these leaders.

Miners and South Africa

It is no coincidence that South Africa has been raised a number of times during the miners' dispute. Arthur Scargill argued that British deep-mined coal is the most economically produced coal in the world except for that produced with *slave labour* in South Africa. But it is British companies and British banks which gain enormous profits from that slave labour in South Africa and British trade unions that have shared in the loot. The failure of the British Labour and trade union movement to oppose British imperialism's backing of the slave labour regime in South Africa has strengthened the very British imperialist state that has now turned against the miners.

The Yorkshire miners' President, Jack Taylor, compared police action against the miners to that used in South Africa and South America, and Scargill has spoken of a paramilitary police exercise. In reality it bears little comparison yet to South Africa where vicious laws herd black people into bantustan concentration camps, separate families, prevent movement anywhere without a pass; where striking and protesting workers are brutally beaten, arrested, shot dead and where their leaders are tortured and murdered in prison. But we must ask what steps have British trade unions taken to prevent subsidiaries of British companies in South Africa calling the South African paramilitary police to disperse, harass and arrest striking workers in South Africa? The capitalist system makes profits out of brutally exploiting people throughout the world. Where democracy and profits come into conflict then democracy will go. The black people in South Africa know this. Oppressed peoples throughout the world know this. British trade unionists are being forced again to understand this.

Miners and Ireland

Jack Taylor, however, could have found comparisons closer to home. In Ireland the British ruling class, using its army and the Royal Ulster Constabulary (RUC), have perfected techniques of 'riot' control, road blocks, legal repression, rigged juryless courts, torture and murder against the Irish people fighting for the basic democratic right to self-determination. In 1981 British trade unionists stood by and watched as ten Irish prisoners of war were murdered on hunger strike. In the same year the same British trade unionists stood by and watched as black and white unemployed youth fought the racist British police on the streets. 4,000 of those involved were arrested and 700 were sent to prison.

1981 uprisings

The failure of British trade unionists to unite with the black people in South Africa against British imperialist backed apartheid, with the Irish people against British imperialist rule, or with the youth of 1981 against the racist British police has aided the strengthening and perfection of the machinery of repression which is now turned against the miners. It allowed the installation of Newman as head of the Metropolitan Police. Newman is undoubtedly masterminding the present national police operation against the miners, drawing on his experience in Ireland.

Arthur Scargill correctly pointed out that:

'Brixton, Toxteth and St Pauls were warning shots that injustice and inequality can only be pushed so far' (*Morning Star* 28 March 1984)

But he should have added that the failure of trade unionists to support the youth has allowed the Thatcher government to attack and defeat

different sections of the working class one by one, because they stood alone. The Socialist Workers Party's (SWP) gross sectarianism forces it to deny this essential point by saying that:

> 'agitation and action among organised workers worries (the Tories) much more than the short-lived eruptions of unemployed youth' (*Socialist Worker* 13 March 1984)

The point is that the eruptions were short-lived precisely because the 'organised workers' refused to support them. The point is that the miners' struggle faces a strengthened and more confident ruling class precisely because of this.

The miners can find real allies and real unity amongst all those sections of the working class, the youth and unemployed, black workers and Irish workers who have already learned who are the friends and who are the enemies of the working class. These forces have no interest in defending the privileged position of either the ruling class or its agents in the working class movement and have every interest in the victory of the striking miners in their struggle for jobs. The miners have much to learn from these forces. Only this unity consistently fought for, not only in the present miners' dispute but in all the battles in the years ahead, can lead the way to the victory of the working class.

30-31 March 1984

Photo: Police attack striking miners at lobby of NUM headquarters, 12 April 1984
John Sturrock/ Network

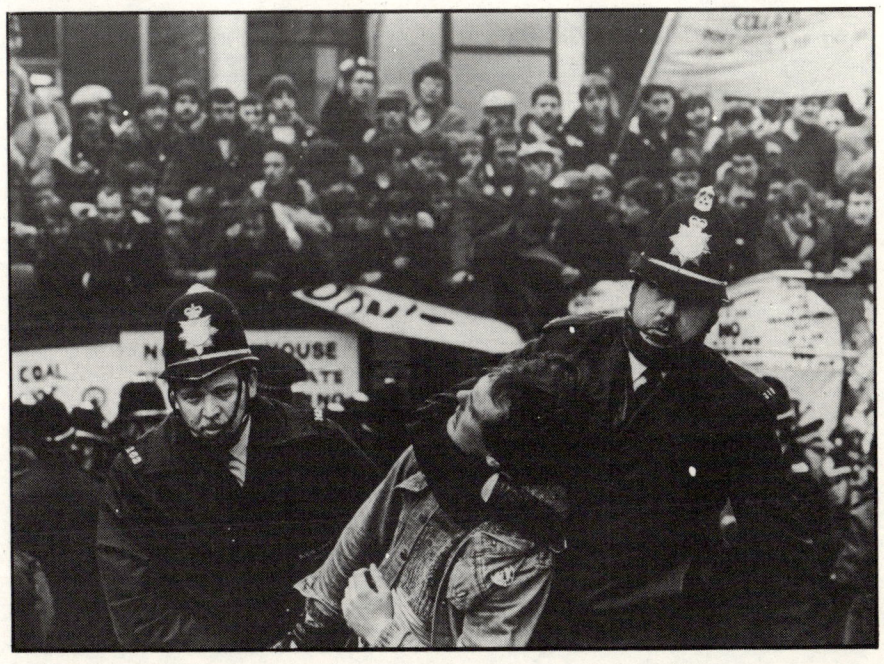

2 MINERS FIGHT POLICE AND SCABS

At the end of the eighth week, the miners' strike continued to demonstrate the growing polarisation in the organised working class movement as the fight of striking miners to defend their jobs reached new levels of bitterness and confrontation. The division in the NUM between the miners whose jobs are under threat and the more privileged miners, particularly in the Nottinghamshire coalfield, had deepened. This was dramatically demonstrated on 1 May when thousands of scab Nottinghamshire miners, protected by mass ranks of police, demonstrated outside their own NUM area office for the 'right to work'. They were confronted by around 2,000 striking miners who had evaded police roadblocks to reach the area office. Bricks and other missiles were exchanged between the two sides. This confrontation showed how deep the split in the NUM had become.

MINERS FIGHT ON

80% of miners are still fighting on, determined, despite increasing hardship, to go on to the bitter end. 120-130 pits are closed and the rest, some 45-55, are kept wholly or partly open by scab miners protected by a massive police operation directed from Scotland Yard. In particular the majority of the 34,000 Nottinghamshire miners, some earning £40-£100 a week more in bonuses than miners in other areas, have turned their backs on their brothers whose jobs are under immediate threat from MacGregor's announcement of 20,000 redundancies. On 1 May the bosses' men of Nottinghamshire were actually *given the day off* on full pay by the NCB to demonstrate their reactionary views at their regional union headquarters, and to demand the resignation of their leaders who had ordered them not to cross picket lines. In the last general election, Sherwood parliamentary constituency which contains some of the most heavily picketed Nottinghamshire pits – Ollerton, Thoresby, Bilsthorpe, Blidworth and Clipstone – returned a Tory MP – a reflection of the relatively high earnings and job security in this area. The current secretary of the Sherwood Labour Party is a miner – he is a scab.

Against the betrayal of 20% of their fellow workers and against a continuous barrage of propaganda from the government, the media and, not least, the Labour Party leaders, the miners, under Scargill's leadership, have decisively rejected a national ballot. 'Stick a ballot, stick a ballot, stick a ballot up your arse...' is one of the derisive theme songs of striking miners. As miners have said time and again: 'We have voted with our feet. Those who want a ballot want to vote against a strike.' And as a South Yorkshire miner said to *Fight Racism! Fight Imperialism!* 'what right does a man have to vote me out of a job?' Following the delegate conference of 19 April which rejected a national ballot and called for national strike action, the continuing determination of the striking miners, was shown on 2 May by the mass picket of over 10,000 at Harworth colliery. That even this display of strength failed to close the pit indicated the scale of the task ahead.

As we have argued, the fundamental feature of this strike is the split in the working class movement. Two issues in particular demonstrate the significance of this split: the conflict at Ravenscraig steel works and the response of the Labour Party to the miners' strike.

RAVENSCRAIG

At Ravenscraig the so-called 'Triple Alliance' of coal, steel and rail unions fell apart in its first real test. Steel workers at the plant on 2 May, following the Scottish NUM decision to curtail coal supplies to Ravenscraig, agreed to use coal brought into the plant by strike-breaking lorry drivers. Ravenscraig shop stewards justified this scabbing as a 'sad and daunting' decision to put their own jobs before those of the miners on strike. Such treachery was encouraged by ISTC leader Bill Sirs. The lorry drivers have so far not responded to an indecisive TGWU instruction to respect the miners' picket line. The outcome of this conflict at Ravenscraig will have a crucial effect on the course of the strike. Of course, it was MacGregor who butchered the steel industry, leaving, as one miner put it, 'a bunch of frightened men'. Instead of drawing together to fight the butchery of a related industry, ISTC leaders, in particular Bill Sirs, have done everything in their power to blame striking miners for future lost steel jobs! Recommending their members to work normally, ISTC leaders have fought to maintain coal imports while trying to deflect attention from their own shameful sell-out of the steel workers.

ISTC scabs

LABOUR BETRAYAL

The miners' strike has revealed Neil Kinnock more and more sharply for the shallow opportunist that he is. At the 10,000 strong rally outside the delegate conference at Sheffield NUM headquarters, Sammy Thompson, Vice-President of Yorkshire NUM, came out with a bitter attack on Kinnock who, he said, had refused to share a platform with him at a meeting in Bolton. 'I'm not getting on the same platform as a Yorkshire miner' Kinnock had said. This disgusting statement reflects the distance which Kinnock and friends feel it necessary to keep from striking miners who have found out that to merely set out on the road to a picket now involves breaking the law. Kinnock has not only called for a national ballot but has also demanded that the

Kinnock refuses to share platform with miner

NUM increase coal supplies to Ravenscraig. On both issues Kinnock has lined up with those workers undermining the miners' strike. Kinnock is only concerned to build his career and backing the miners, he believes, will not help him in his task. The Labour NEC has launched a 50p levy per member per week for the miners. Coming some seven weeks into the dispute, for leaders like Kinnock, this is a sop to cover the shame of their betrayal.

Photo: Striking miners reject national ballot, NUM headquarters, 12 April 1984 John Sturrock/ Network

HARDSHIP GROWS

Every means of attack has been brought against the striking miners and their families – to force them into submission. An imaginary £15 a week strike pay which miners *do not* receive from the NUM, is deducted from benefit paid to strikers' families. An average family receives about £20 a week and a single man nothing at all. One Barnsley family stated that due to the wife's £12 a week part-time job, only £4.50 a week benefit was being paid. The most recent turn of the screw is the instruction to the DHSS to deduct from benefit any loans that have been made by local authorities to assist miners' families with electricity and gas bills. In Barnsley a young miner is due to be evicted by the building society.

The NUM does not give strike pay – they say that their millions of pounds of assets and investments would be gone in a matter of weeks if they did.

Women organise

Despite the hardships, the media has been unable to drive a wedge between the miners and their families and communities. Women have joined picket lines, organised demonstrations in working areas, formed committees, provided meals for families. As one North Derby-

22

shire miner said, 'Let MacGregor carry on with his steaks, we'll carry on with our baked beans to the end'. Pickets have been labelled 'Scargill's Red Guards...' and accused of spreading 'their menacing lawlessness across Britain' (*The Observer*). Yet, as one Durham miner, who was due to receive £20,000 in redundancy money if he agreed to sell his job, said: '£20,000 is 4 years wages. After that there's 25 years on the dole. Who wants that?' In the North East, in some of the mining villages where pits have already closed, unemployment is 40%, and 60% among 18-23 year olds. The nearest towns are places like Consett, themselves devastated by unemployment.

POLICE KEEP PITS OPEN

While Thatcher and Co refuse to raise subsidies to keep miners in jobs, they are happy to pay the political price of at least £2 million per week for policing to defeat the strike. Nottinghamshire County Council had, by the end of April, already spent £13.9 million of its £42 million annual police budget. Only the massive scale of the centralised police operation has kept the working pits open. The ruling class is using the lessons learned in Ireland and during the 1981 uprisings. Police have even been flown by Boeing Jet from Hampshire to Nottinghamshire, at a cost of £10,000, to provide reinforcements. As Tony Benn stated in Parliament, 'I believe that what the government has done is to bring the police tactics of Northern Ireland into the heart of Britain.' More and more brazenly the police have employed road blocks, political questioning, beatings, illegal fingerprinting and photographing, snatch squads, phone-taps and infiltration. The number of arrests had climbed to 1,479 by 2 May with many miners being forced to accept bail conditions forbidding them to go near NCB premises. Four miners, who had already been arrested and bailed on these conditions, were rearrested for merely driving down the M1, and charged with breach of the peace. The magistrate refused bail and they were remanded in Lincoln prison. A picket of hundreds of miners was told by the prison governor that the four were being treated like any other prisoners. What an assurance!

Miners are being beaten up daily by the police. 70 were beaten up in a truncheon attack in Sheffield after the 10,000 strong rally outside the NUM headquarters on 19 April. As one young Yorkshire miner told *Fight Racism! Fight Imperialism!*, 'The Mets have been sent to kick the shit out of us'. Union leaders have been arrested – the President and Vice-President of Derbyshire NUM, and Jim Colgan, Midlands General Secretary who was detained and beaten, and only released when police found out who he was. At Bevercotes, Nottingham, a Scottish miner was picked up by the police, taken into the woods and beaten up. He was left with badly bruised legs and cracked ribs. The police said to him 'if we can't get you one way, we'll get you another' (*Socialist Worker*).

Miners attacked Sheffield 19 April 1984

The South Wales Chief Constable has admitted using infiltrators, and a policeman dressed as a miner was shown on ITN news pointing out people to be arrested. One South Wales coach firm operator

Surveillance and infiltration

Clayton Jones, after receiving a call from the local NUM about a coach, was phoned by Derbyshire police asking him for the precise destination! The Post Office Engineers Union has said that Home Office denials of phone tapping are 'laughable'. Groups of miners have been interrogated by police on their political views – would they vote Conservative or Communist? Did they vote for Scargill? Yet again the police are playing a directly political role.

The massive police operation and systematic brutality against striking miners is exposing to many trade unionists the brutal reality of the British imperialist ruling class and its state – a reality long recognised by black workers, Irish workers and others who have suffered imperialist repression and racism. The scale of the state's attack on the miners results from the refusal of the striking miners to allow their fight to be sabotaged by the more privileged sections of their own union or by the treachery of other sections of the Labour and trade union movement. And as the struggle has gone on, the split in the working class movement has widened. Such a polarisation is inevitable.

The British middle class left's position on this issue, as on all others, reflects its class position. They refuse to recognise the political reality of a working class divided by privilege and sectionalism. So

---

'Brixton, Toxteth and St Pauls were warning shots that injustice and inequality can only be pushed so far.'
Arthur Scargill March 1984

SWP and miners

Socialist Worker at first believed that the solution to 'disunity' was more and better political argument and propaganda by rank and file workers directed at the Nottingham rank and file miners. Now after many weeks of harsh reality proving them wrong they are reduced to saying:

'It will not be easy to win them (Nottingham miners) for the strike, and it would be folly to stake the whole future of the strike on doing so.

The strike can still be made to bite, even if a substantial number of Notts miners continue to scab – but only if picketing is stepped up generally – outside power stations, steel works, coal and coke depots.' (*Socialist Worker* 5 May 1984).

When reality contradicts their middle class idealism the Socialist Workers Party simply runs away from the problem. Their remarks show that they have no understanding of what is at stake. For at Ravenscraig, a major steel works, the striking miners face fundamentally the same political problem as they face in Nottingham – a divided working class.

RCP calls for ballot

The Revolutionary Communist Party's (RCP) refusal to recognise the split in the working class movement has taken them right into the camp of reaction. They have 'launched' a campaign for a national

24

ballot as the only way to 'unify' all miners, scabs and strikers alike. The RCP has no base amongst any workers let alone miners. But with typically British middle class arrogance have refused to listen to what any striking miner has understood from the very beginning of the strike. That a national ballot serves *only* the interests of Thatcher, the National Coal Board, the opportunist scoundrel Kinnock, and those miners scabbing on the strike. So far from any political reality is this middle class sect, that it regards the decision, taken at the 19 April delegate conference, to make easier the calling of national strike action by reducing the majority needed (from 55% to a simple majority) as 'manipulating the rules' (*The Next Step*). Need any more be said?

The fundamental point that the miners' strike is driving home is that the tactics of the strike must be based on the interests of the miners under threat and not the interests of the more privileged sections of the union. The failure of the majority of Nottinghamshire miners, or indeed the Ravenscraig steel workers, to support the strike cannot be explained away on the grounds of 'insufficient propaganda' or 'lack of political argument', but *represents a real clash of material interests.* They are determined to hold on to the jobs they have rather than fight for the jobs of all workers.

The miners fighting to defend their jobs face an alliance of the government and its police thugs, Labour Party and trade union opportunists, and workers who refuse to go beyond their own narrow sectional interests. One of the political lessons of this strike is that the traditional methods and structures of the existing organised trade union movement, dominated as it is by opportunism and the interests of its more privileged sections, cannot defend the miners or indeed any other section of the working class forced to fight to survive. It is the determination of the striking miners to defend their jobs which is bringing home this reality.

4-5 May 1984

3 POLICE RIOT MINERS FIGHT ON

Kinnock scabs

As the twelfth week of the miners' strike drew to a close it was clear that all the lying propaganda, the massive police operation and the sabotage by sections of the trade union movement had failed to undermine the determination of the striking miners. The ruling class responded to this with a systematic escalation of police violence. Every day that the strike continued it exposed more and more openly the real character of imperialist 'democracy' and political power. Police, laws, courts and prisons—not the ballot box—are the real weapons with which the ruling class seeks to impose its will. Ruling class power rests on 'special bodies of armed men' and a state apparatus answerable only to the class which employs and controls them.

STATE VIOLENCE ESCALATES

'The police are everywhere. It's just like Belfast' (Ollerton miner, quoted in The Observer)

Orgreave Nearly 3,200 arrests have now been made – over one thousand in the ten days up to 31 May. The most dramatic confrontation between miners and police took place on 29/30/31 May at the Orgreave coke depot near Sheffield. For the first time, police riot gear, developed in Ireland and used in the 1981 uprisings, was deployed in an industrial dispute. Mounted police wielding truncheons and batons have charged picket lines and hounded miners over fields. Police wearing full riot gear and using dogs have viciously attacked pickets.

In Nottinghamshire police operations have been particularly intense in order to intimidate and prevent pickets from Yorkshire and elsewhere from reinforcing the Notts miners out on strike. Pit villages have been flooded with police, including special squads of plain clothes police thugs, under the guise of investigating 'intimidation' of scab miners. Thatcher knows that as the strike proceeds large scale production of coal from the Nottinghamshire miners will be more and more vital to maintain power supplies. That is why Nottinghamshire is virtually under police occupation.

26

On 17 May police laid siege for seventeen hours to Blidworth, a mining village in Nottinghamshire. People were prevented from leaving their homes, phones were cut off and the entire area was sealed off by police roadblocks. Yorkshire pickets being put up in the homes and gardens of striking Notts miners found police searching their tents and belongings. When they protested a miner was punched to the ground and arrested and others were threatened with arrest if they left their homes. Squads of police conducted searches of homes demanding proof of identity of the occupants.

The NUM has gathered together a catalogue of police crimes, cowardly beatings of pickets, phone tapping and of plain clothes police acting as *agents provocateurs*. One Scottish miner, Robert Malone, was kidnapped by plain clothes police in Ollerton, Nottinghamshire on his way to picket duty, driven miles into the countryside, beaten up with a cosh or truncheon and then abandoned with his injuries and told 'you have found your way down here and you will find your fucking way home'. One new development has been the sighting by miners of relatives known to be in the army, dressed up as police – for example a miner saw his brother, supposedly on active service in the North of Ireland, dressed as a policeman at Harworth colliery in Notts.

Blidworth besieged

Photo: Riot police and mounted police, Orgreave, 29 May 1984 John Harris/IFL

27

Miners demonstration in Mansfield, Nottinghamshire, 14 May 1984

The first striking thing about 14 May was the massive size of the demonstration—45,000 was claimed by the NUM. Over 80% of the marchers were miners or miners' wives and families. The demonstrators were all firmly behind the strike and Arthur Scargill. The most popular slogans were against MacGregor and the national ballot. There was a general feeling of hostility towards the police with plenty of chants of 'Sieg Heil!' directed at individual police officers.

The march wound its way through Mansfield ending with a rally. Arthur Scargill made a speech calling for a Labour government. The response he got from the miners when he spoke amounted to hero worship.

As soon as the rally finished, after Scargill had spoken, the stewards disappeared and the police took over, organising the bringing of the miners' coaches into the car park where the rally had taken place. About one hour after the end of the rally the confrontation with the police began. Two police attempted to arrest a miner and were attacked by other miners who freed their comrade. Young miners quickly began to assemble and attack the police who only numbered about a dozen at that moment. What looked like a special patrol unit in a transit roared on to the car park behind the crowd of young miners and made a 'snatch' of at least two miners. The young miners were urging others to get off the coaches and fight the police but it was too late, and the police began to advance through the car park. There were more skirmishes and the police beat up a young miner next to our coach. They held our coach on the car park until nearly all the others had left and arrested someone on our coach.

The strength of the demonstration was in the massive support it had from the mining communities. Its weakness was the lack of support from elsewhere, and the abandoning of the demonstrators at the end of the rally.

Miners and the courts

In line with the government's overall strategy, legitimate trade union activity, the right to picket, demonstrate and protest is being criminalised. For the first time, five miners were charged with 'conspiracy', and, more seriously, fifty were charged with 'riot' after police attacked miners after the massive Mansfield rally on 14 May where they beat a man unconscious. Riot charges, which must be tried in the Crown Court, carry unlimited fines or gaol sentences. On 31 May and 1 June, twenty-nine miners were arrested at Orgreave and charged with 'unlawful assembly' – a charge used in Liverpool 8 in 1981, carrying unlimited penalties.

The courts have continued this criminalisation process by imposing, in nearly every case, bail conditions which make further picketing a criminal offence. Even miners facing trivial charges such as obstruction have had these bail conditions imposed. In some cases the conditions virtually amount to house arrest. The Kent NUM leader, Malcolm Pitt was imprisoned in Canterbury gaol after defying such bail conditions. He spent three weeks in prison merely for the charge of obstruction. When he appeared in court he was handcuffed to a prison screw. Scargill, himself arrested for obstruction on his third day

28

at the Orgreave coke depot on 30 May, has called the police a 'Nazi gestapo' and accused them of using 'open terror tactics' akin to those in a 'Latin American police state'.

Scab miners have been able to use the courts to intervene directly in the affairs of the NUM. No election or ballot was involved here, just a couple of reactionary judges working for the government. Three miners from Sherwood Colliery have actually succeeded in getting the courts to declare the Notts area strike as unofficial. As Scargill said, such a decision by the court was 'consistent with over a century of anti-working class judgements'. 1,500 Lancashire miners, suspended from the union for five years by their area leaders, have continued to cross picket lines and have succeeded in getting the High Court to declare their suspension illegal.

NEW FORMS OF RESISTANCE

'The scene was as dramatic as almost any during the Toxteth and Brixton rioting' (The Guardian report on Orgreave)

At the start of the strike we argued that 'only by going beyond legal, constitutional and traditional methods of trade union struggle can such a fight be won'. In the face of massive police violence the miners have been quick to show this in practice. Mass picketing has been maintained in spite of police road blocks and the sealing off of whole areas. Police attacks are now being forcefully resisted. After the arrest of Arthur Scargill at Orgreave on 30 May a Portakabin was dragged across the road as a barricade and set alight. Telegraph poles and torn-up paving stones were used by miners to attack police lines. Wire was strung at neck height between lamp posts in the path of a mounted police charge. Kent miners from Betteshanger colliery occupied the NCB headquarters at Hobart House in London in protest at Scargill's arrest and the continued detention of Malcolm Pitt. Among their demands, broadcast from the first floor window, was a call to 'smash the police state'.

The arrest of Anne Scargill on 16 May highlighted what has been a very significant development in the strike: the increasingly militant role of women – not just in providing back-up services but in organising and participating in pickets. Organised groups of women are multiplying rapidly – 10,000 women marched through Barnsley on 12 May. Groups of women go out picketing regularly – often to replace men restricted by bail conditions. All-women mass pickets have been held. The women state they are determined to show they are shoulder to shoulder with the men – in standing up to the police and in their willingness to be arrested. At the same time, the organisation of food parcels and kitchens, collections and advice centres are now the mining communities' means of survival as the government squeezes strikers' families harder and harder. The vicious Rhodes Boyson, then Social Security minister, made it clear that even firewood and food parcels can be deducted from benefits.

The courage and determination of the Greenham Common women is regarded by these women as an inspiration. A group of Barnsley

Anne Scargill arrested

29

women against pit closures said that it would be worthwhile to go to Greenham to see how they have learnt to handle the police – 'we could learn a lot'.

DIVISIONS DEEPEN

'They are hiding behind the ballot call. Many of them are spineless gits. They've got big cars, videos and freezers. They own their own homes and want to live in Nob Row'. (Young miner from Ollerton, Notts about the scabs in The Observer)

Despite the continuing mass pickets and pickets by Notts strikers, the greater proportion of Notts miners continue to cross picket lines. Support for the miners' struggle has also failed to materialise in any sustained form from the trade union movement. Rather the strike has exposed the depth of the divisions in the labour movement. Nowhere has this been shown more clearly than in the battles fought over the Ravenscraig and Scunthorpe steelworks. ISTC members, egged on by their reactionary leader Bill Sirs, helped non-union labour to unload a shipload of coal at Hunterston – enough to keep Ravenscraig going for several weeks. Bosses' man Sirs said 'steel workers will use any materials brought in by the BSC (British Steel Corporation)'. This scabbing, and a massive police operation, was able to undermine the stand of the Scottish miners who had been sick to the teeth at the fact that production at Ravenscraig was being allowed to continue as normal.

Triple Alliance crumbles

The 'Triple Alliance' of steel, transport and mining unions has been rent apart. Only some dockers, seamen and railway workers have shown any real solidarity. The NUR and ASLEF were to have begun an overtime ban in support of their pay claim but were offered 4.9-5.6% which they accepted. The power workers – whose support could have brought the strike to a swift conclusion – applauded their leader Eric Hammond at their conference when he called Scargill a 'nursery revolutionary' and said 'we won't use trade union power to bring down elected government'. It is no surprise that this reactionary has just concluded a no-strike agreement with Nissan in their new factory.

Murray sabotages support

TUC leader Len Murray stepped into the strike in order to directly and openly sabotage a Yorkshire and Humberside Day of Action called in support of the miners. He ordered union leaders point blank to call the action off, saying that it was against the TUC constitution. Murray has also stated that he may not resign in September if no 'suitable' candidate has been found, ie he feels he may still be needed to sabotage the miners' struggle. Despite Murray's intervention, large numbers of workers struck on the Day of Action – buses in Barnsley and Doncaster stopped; all trains were stopped through Sheffield and Doncaster; many workers from the National and Local Government Officers Association (NALGO) and hospital ancillary workers came out. Firemen and ambulance workers answered 999 calls only; 1,000 dockers took some action and a few factories closed. The Scottish TUC, which had passed a motion for a day of action on 9 May with many fine words spoken in support of the miners, then proceeded to

30

Police harassment in Blidworth

As told to FRFI by Doreen Humber—striker's wife

After the 14 May Mansfield rally we had about 60 Yorkshire miners staying here, in mine and the two houses next door. We had some of them staying in tents and caravans in our back gardens. They were going home to Yorkshire on Thursday so on Wednesday night we went out for a farewell drink. The police were in and out of the pub all the time and there was a scab in there who phoned the police and said 'there are 20 pickets waiting to beat me up', which was a complete lie. We went home and went into Annette's house for a coffee and to have a talk. We wanted some sandwiches and one of the Yorkshire lads said he had bread in his tent and would get it. When he went out he saw a copper coming out of the tent and the police were banging on people's doors. They said there had been a phone call about a disturbance—there was not any disturbance. The police had insisted on searching Doreen's house while there was only a 14 year old in there babysitting. She was upset and crying. The police pushed one of the Yorkshire lads out of the drive and beat him up—he had cracked ribs and an injured shoulder.

The next thing was 13 police vans came. One of the coppers had dropped his torch while searching the tent and they wanted it back. A couple of streets away 250 coppers were being marched up the road. We managed to get a phone call through to our solicitor but he was stopped from coming into the area by the police. Our phone went dead then and we couldn't make any calls out. All night police vans were going past the house every three minutes.

Next day the whole thing was reported on the TV. At 1.30pm the police came back and said they wanted to arrest us and the Yorkshire lads. 2 police came to my door and asked me questions about my car and my husband Philip came home then and they questioned him. The police went when they saw TV cameras coming up the street. When the Yorkshire lads left to go home the police threatened to get me. The very next day while two reporters were here in the Welfare centre a young lad was attacked by a scab just outside. The police grabbed the striker and then they grabbed my son David who's just 17. They said 'Doreen Humber's lad—we've got him'. They tried to get into the Welfare centre but we shut the door so they broke in and trapped a girl's arm in the door. They charged David with 'breach of the peace and obstruction'. In court they said he had been harbouring Yorkshire pickets in the garden!

Then on Bank Holiday Monday we went for a drink and a scab attacked one of us, Ken. Anyway we all went home and then about 1.45am the police came to our houses. they arrested our husbands 'on suspicion of assault'. They kept Philip and Alan for 32 hours and John and Ken for 36 hours. John and Ken were charged with 'malicious wounding'. They were trying to do them for stealing the police torch but it's now with our lawyers as evidence. I've had to take out an injunction against the police now. They know that if they can smash me they can smash us. I've been travelling around raising the money for the Welfare centre.

The police are even stopping and questioning young children and saying 'Where's your dad—he'll be locked up next week'.

We won't be forced back—we will win. Now is the time to stand up and fight, you can't keep lying back and taking it. I've never been political before but how that woman Thatcher is still walking around I'll never know.

try and sabotage it by calling for 'individuals' to take action. A large march still took place in Glasgow. In fact the miners have received more significant solidarity action from the official trade union movement abroad than they have from the TUC. In Australia, which provides the biggest share of Britain's coal imports, mining and dockers' unions have refused to send any coal to Britain.

Concannon and Reid scab

Leading Labour MPs are still refusing to openly side with striking miners – only 60 signed a recent motion of support. Don Concannon, Labour MP for Mansfield, Notts – who went to visit Bobby Sands when he was dying on hunger strike to tell him that the Labour Party did not support him – sided with Leon Brittan when he condemned so-called 'intimidation' of scab miners. Dennis Skinner MP aptly called him a 'copper's nark'! Jimmy Reid, former leader of the Upper Clyde Shipyard occupation, ex-Communist Party and now member of the Labour Party, appearing on *Union World* on Channel 4, compared young miners to the National Front and attacked Arthur Scargill. As the strike has deepened Kinnock and Stan Orme have made every effort to pressurise Scargill into a compromise. Kinnock has constantly begged Thatcher to intervene in the strike (!), talking of the 'continuing agony' of the strike. Certainly *he* is in 'continuing agony' as increased repression has brought about an increased willingness on the part of miners to fight the police and go beyond constitutional methods of struggle. Kinnock is still wittering on about democracy and a national ballot when mounted police are batoning pickets, and police are forcing their way into miners' homes, and sealing off whole areas.

Photo: Miners build a barricade and set fire to a Portakabin at Orgreave

After the miners forcefully resisted police attacks at Orgreave, Kinnock quickly condemned them. He said that there was no place in any industrial dispute for missiles, battering rams or other acts of violence. He went on:

'The miners, like all other British trade unionists, understand that their real strength comes from peaceful organisation, peaceful protest and peaceful picketing.'

On the contrary! The miners have seen their peaceful methods of struggle met by huge attacks by the police and courts. Many have seen that they can only defend their rights and pursue their struggle by going beyond peaceful, constitutional means. Kinnock and the Labour Party are now attempting to isolate these militant miners by raising the spectre of 'violence'. The press and TV are aiding this by concentrating on interviewing miners opposed to 'violence'. In the face of this, Scargill, to his credit, has refused to be drawn into any condemnation of the miners' methods of struggle and has consistently attacked police repression and brutality.

HARD LESSONS FROM THE MINERS' STRIKE

'There's quiet lads in this village now that hate the police and are thinking of joining revolutionary groups' (Fife miner, quoted in the Financial Times)

When *Fight Racism! Fight Imperialism!* is sold to striking miners they often ask what has Ireland, South Africa, imperialism and racism to do with us? The answers to these questions are already being thrown up in the course of the miners' struggle. It is miners themselves who have made the connection between their own bail conditions and house arrest of political activists in apartheid South Africa. It is they who have compared police stopping miners travelling outside their own areas with the pass law system in South Africa. They have realised that coal produced under slave labour conditions in South Africa will be used to undermine their struggle here. In other words, they are being forced to learn the lesson that they have an interest in common with the black miners in South Africa to destroy the British imperialist-backed racist apartheid state.

It is miners themselves who talk of a growing police state. Some are drawing comparisons between the police operation against the miners and that against the nationalist minority in the Six Counties of Ireland. Some recognise that the lessons the police learned from putting down the 1981 uprisings of black and white youth on the streets of British cities are being used against them today. They have yet to draw the political conclusion that to defend themselves they must stand in solidarity with these struggles against the British imperialist state. But the more state repression against the miners escalates, the more they will have no choice but to turn to methods of struggle used on the streets of Belfast and in the 1981 uprisings.

Finally, and most importantly, the miners' struggle has shown up those forces in the working class which will not support them. They are seeing in practice that imperialism splits the working class movement and creates privileged layers within it. These layers have no interest in taking any action which will undermine the system in any way. That is why the Labour Party, the TUC and major trade unions have failed to give active support to the miners.

The ruling class and its allies are now becoming increasingly concerned that if the miners' struggle goes on a whole section of workers will begin to see the need for rebuilding the working class movement in Britain on a revolutionary basis. It is this fact that is making sections of the ruling class less certain of the wisdom of starving the miners back to work and more open to finding a compromise. The National Coal Board has been forced to begin talks with the miners' executive to see if an 'acceptable' compromise can be found. However, any concessions made by the Coal Board will result from the determination of the striking miners and the mining communities to carry this struggle through to the bitter end.

1-2 June 1984

Orgreave, 30 May 1984

We arrived at Orgreave at about 10.15am. We spoke to a group of miners who told us that Scargill's arrest had taken place before 8am and three others had been arrested with him. There had also been some trouble during the first run of lorries at about 9am. They had seen two pickets dragged off and beaten up. Police had also charged up and down on horseback and had been bricked. There were only about 1,000 pickets there, the majority of them hemmed in by the police in a field in front of the coke depot. The previous day there had been at least 5,000 miners and the general feeling was that they had been outnumbered by the police, some even said by 5 to 1. The miners also mentioned that contrary to press lies the cop who had broken a leg the previous day, had not been dragged from his horse by miners, but that a police van had run into the side of the horse which had trampled on its rider.

We spoke to three young miners who described the day before as 'just like Belfast'. At about 1pm miners started arriving from nowhere and moved down to the depot. Across the bottom of the hill in front of the depot were mass ranks of police, some with horses, some in a field with dogs. There was quite a gap between police and miners. Soon bricks began flying. A police officer said over a loudhailer: 'These tactics are getting you nowhere'. Some miners tried to roll a telegraph pole down the hill to loud cheers. A wire was strung across the road to stop the mounted police. A barricade was erected at the point the police had charged up to. The barricade consisted of telegraph poles, bricks, rocks, stones, and fencing. Barbed wire was added—more cheers. A Portakabin was rolled from a nearby field into the road and set alight. Stones were gathered at the barricade.

Soon we heard the sound of horses charging. The horses appeared at the top of the hill but did not advance any further. The horses had come all the way from the depot. The miners still down there had presumably scattered and about 10 had been arrested.

Some miners started to break up a wall in case the police advanced further. A police van suddenly appeared and waves of missiles hit it—and bounced off the perspex windows. People were getting frustrated and a couple of other vehicles were hit. Then everyone melted away and disappeared.

BELFAST COMES TO BLIDWORTH

The effectiveness of the miners' strike and the determination of the miners and their communities to fight on began to create divisions among the ruling class. While Thatcher remained intransigent and eager to pursue the crusade against Scargill and the NUM, other sections of the ruling class were becoming increasingly aware of the dangers of the strike continuing. The British economy, already very vulnerable to any added international and domestic pressures, suffered the double blow of rapidly rising international interest rates and the sudden outbreak of a national docks strike. Little wonder that Thatcher's leadership was being called into question by her previous allies. Not only was the miners' strike threatening further economic damage but, more significantly, it posed a serious challenge to the political legitimacy of the British state, its police, courts and other institutions. And in doing this it inevitably represented a threat to the traditional leadership of the Labour and trade union movement, the vast majority of whom scabbed on the miners' strike.

NCB forced to talk

Under growing pressures arising from the determined fight of the miners the NCB has been forced to engage in serious talks. The NCB has, after eighteen weeks, apparently begun to backtrack on its pit closure programme. Thatcher's and MacGregor's intention to smash the miners and decimate their communities is foundering on the rock of the miners' resistance.

The outcome of the strike rests on the continuing determination and sacrifice of the miners and their communities. On the one side, the ruling class has ranged its whole apparatus of police and courts against the miners; with whole sections of the trade union movement, as in the case of the steel workers, giving their support to Thatcher and MacGregor by continuing to work; the Labour Party has offered only token opposition to Thatcher. On the other side, the ruling class is up against not only the determination and militancy of the miners, but also of the women, whose organisation of their communities, aided by countrywide support in terms of food and money, has enabled the strike to hold out.

STATE REPRESSION

Arrests are now approaching 4,000, with an increasing number of miners facing charges such as 'illegal assembly' and 'riotous

Newstead

A young Notts miner, Mark Brierley and his brother were held for 12 days in Lincoln Prison. They were arrested outside Mark's NCB home, which he was decorating before his forthcoming marriage. Mark, who had been arrested previously during the strike for shouting 'scab' on the picket line, was already on bail conditions which restricted him to picketing at the Newstead pit. On the day of his arrest the police approached him and demanded that he move his car which was parked outside his home. When he questioned this he was assaulted by the police, who pushed him to the ground and stood on his arms and legs. His brother rushed out to see what was happening and was also arrested. Both were handcuffed so tightly that the police could not unlock the cuffs and had to call to the pit blacksmith to cut the cuffs off.

When Martin and his brother appeared in court the police opposed bail and the magistrate put them both in Lincoln prison. Finally after 12 days his lawyers were able to get bail granted but on condition that Martin does not go back to his new house.

The Newstead miners who told FRFI about this case had witnessed Martin and his brother's arrest. They felt it was one of the worst cases they had seen. Local strikers mounted a 200-strong picket outside Lincoln prison on 29 June.

assembly' – all of which carry the threat of prison sentences. Another miner – Joe Green – has been killed on picket duty. Massive roadblock operations continue to seal off Nottinghamshire from pickets: on 28 June 1,900 miners in 475 cars were turned back – 2,000 got through. On the same day police turned back 1,200 pickets from the Scunthorpe area. Whole towns are sealed off at a moment's notice.

Such is the determination of the government to keep Notts and other working mines open that each such mine has a permanently allocated police support unit (PSU). Each PSU consists of three sections of ten officers, sergeants and an inspector. They are all specially trained riot police with equipment standardised on a country-wide basis. The use of well practised manoeuvres such as snatch squads operating in V-formation have become commonplace, as is the sight of police doing military style drill in pit yards.

As pressure has increased on the ruling class to keep up supplies to steelworks, the police have launched brutal attacks against pickets. On 18 June at Orgreave coke depot in South Yorkshire, scene of previous battles, riot police and cavalry charges were launched against miners with unprecedented ferocity. Scores of miners were attacked including Arthur Scargill. Miners had to meet force with force: barricades were built and cars were commandeered and burnt. Stakes were driven into the road to stop police horse charges. Police snatch squads were ordered to 'take prisoners', attacking in V-formations, and were heard cheering and clapping as wounded pickets were dragged off to police vans.

Political bail conditions and curfews

A lesson learned by the oppressed in the Six Counties of Ireland is that beneath the mask of 'democracy' the British state consists of a relentless machinery of police, courts and prisons which it sets into motion against those who try to fight it. Blanket bail conditions (imposed in 3,000 cases by the end of June), forcible photographing, fingerprinting, the use of curfews, and the corrupt alliance of police, magistrates and solicitors, are the means being used to criminalise the most militant miners. By these means, police are also massing intelligence while physically reducing the number of miners available for picketing. Breaking of bail conditions means prison – several miners and NUM officials have spent time in prison for this reason.

Mansfield in Notts has become a centre for mass trials and detentions. Courts are held as late as midnight with only the defendants, a duty solicitor, a CID sergeant, prosecution and magistrate present. Bail conditions – which forbid miners to take part in any activity connected with the strike, including demonstrations, rallies and pickets anywhere except their own place of work – are distributed in duplicated form. When challenged on 5 July by solicitor Gareth Pearce, representing a group of miners, the chairman of the bench refused to see any reason for changing their bail conditions and proceeded to issue the same duplicated bail conditions.

Curfews on striking Notts miners from 9pm to 7am are widespread. With renewed NCB attempts to get North Derbyshire men back to work, four Derbyshire strikers have been issued with curfews of 1pm to 9am – 20 hours! This amounts to virtual house arrest.

The ruling class is tireless in its efforts to beat the strike. Their attempts to smash the strike have been coordinated at the highest government level. A leak to the *Daily Mirror* recently exposed the government's involvement in the deal that settled the railway workers' wage claim. While unable to find the money to keep open pits, or to fund the National Health Service, Thatcher has endless resources to devote to smashing the NUM. Scargill has stated that the dispute has now cost more than the Falklands War. A leading City firm of stockbrokers estimated the cost at over £1 billion. BSC (on whose board MacGregor still sits) is funding convoys of lorries to carry iron ore at a cost of £50,000 per day, while the NCB pays £½ million for a series of lying advertisements in the press.

International solidarity

From: the Miners' Union of Nicaragua affiliated to the Sandinista Workers' Confederation

To: Brother miners of Great Britain

Dear Comrades,

A revolutionary Sandinista greeting from the mineworkers of Nicaragua!

Through this letter we, the miners of Nicaragua, would like to assure you of our solidarity with the struggle you are waging in your country to win trade union democracy to sustain your struggle without your rights being suppressed.

Brothers, we would like to tell you not to lose heart; right and reason will win through when there is a willpower as strong as yours.

We know you are confronting reactionaries, conservatives and right-wingers led by the IRON WOMAN—MARGARET THATCHER—but your struggle is just, and being just will win, as the old reactionary structures of capitalism are swept away by the incontainable force of the revolutionary progressive ideas of the organised and conscious working class, guided by the best sons of the proletariat.

Forward, Brother British Miners! Your brother miners in Nicaragua support your just struggle, a struggle which will be long, cruel and full of sacrifices, but we say to you, brothers: THE STRUGGLE CONTINUES, VICTORY IS CERTAIN, 'FREE COUNTRY OR DEATH'

signed ENOC CASTELLON
for the Union of Mineworkers 'Pedro Roque V.', El Limon Mine, Nicaragua

WORKING CLASS DIVIDED

The strike has continued to polarise the working class and to expose ever more clearly those who will not support the miners. At the forefront of those turning their backs on the miners are the steel workers. Faced with the threatened blockade of steel plants, ISTC officials stated at their union conference on 24 June, 'we will carry coal in on our backs to save the plants'. The ISTC conference discussion of the miners' request for support was dominated by BSC Deputy Chairman Bob Scholey, who said BSC would not accept any 'managerially unacceptable' agreement between miners and steelworkers. Bill Sirs, ISTC leader, said that the steel men would have to abide by this decision. Further, when Sirs suggested a 50% production level and Scholey insisted on 70%, the latter was backed by the conference.

Railway workers boycott coal

Railway workers have almost completely stopped coal and ore trains into Llanwern, Scunthorpe and Ravenscraig. This in turn has brought about the increase in scab lorry convoys – driven at murderous speed past picket lines. At Llanwern, where pickets battled with police, lorries in convoys of more than 100 in both directions, were drawn from firms as far apart as Notts and Exeter. The TGWU has at last taken the decision to expel fourteen of their members who are drivers from Hazell Transport, in Newport, one of the main firms organising the scab convoys.

First docks strike

National Union of Seamen members have continued to blockade the import of coal. On 9 July the TGWU called a national dock workers strike after the unloading of iron ore by scab labour at Immingham near Scunthorpe for use by BSC. The length of this strike could have a critical impact on the miners' strike.

Notts scabs threaten breakaway union

At the same time the scab miners of Notts, three quarters of whom are working, are in the process of forming, with the NCB's blessing, a breakaway union – whose leaders are reportedly rushing to join the SDP/Liberal Alliance. The Notts scabs have received the full backing of the courts, with the High Court even ruling that the NUM conference could not discuss the new disciplinary and expulsion rules which the scabs fear. Scargill and the NUM conference treated the court's reactionary judgement with the contempt it deserved.

LABOUR PARTY

Whilst the striking miners have continued their bitter struggle for four and a half months, Labour MPs have hardly disturbed the tranquility of the House of Commons. Thatcher has faced no serious threat from a Labour opposition which she knows has not, with a few honourable exceptions, supported the striking miners. Spineless windbag, Kinnock, has repeatedly called on Thatcher to intervene in the strike – precisely what she and her blue-uniformed thugs have been doing all along! After the battle against police at Orgreave on 18 June, Kinnock said that the scenes there were 'horrifying, untypical and unBritish'. No doubt like similar scenes in the Six Counties of Ireland. The left Labour MPs, whilst supporting the miners, will not push the Labour Party for open support as this would expose the vast number of scabs within its ranks. Thus Tony Benn withdrew a motion to the Labour Party National Executive Committee calling for national demonstrations in favour of a vague one calling for discussions with the NUM with the view to organising a joint national campaign against pit closures.

38

MINERS RESISTANCE—THE LESSONS LEARNED

Photo: Police charge picketing miners, Orgreave, 18 June 1984 John Sturrock/ Network

... acts of terrorism without the bullet and the bomb'. James Anderton, Chief Constable of Manchester, on mass pickets.

The scale of state repression has forced the striking miners to go beyond legal, constitutional and peaceful methods of struggle. The ruling class, which has denied the miners their basic democratic rights, has now begun accusing them of terrorism. The miners are learning the lessons which the Irish people and oppressed people throughout the world have learned – that they have no choice but to fight and that they will be branded as criminals and terrorists when they do so. The anger of striking miners, after eighteen weeks of police beatings, spying and harassment, has reached boiling point. Police stations in Maltby, Goldthorpe and Hemsworth have been stoned and besieged. At Rossington colliery (near Doncaster) an NCB van was set on fire and used as a barricade in order to besiege managers carrying out work against the wishes of the NUM. Similar attacks on NCB property took place in Fitzwilliam on the night of 9 July and were the result of anger against police provocation. Barricades have also been used at Orgreave to defend pickets from rampaging mobs of police. Prevented by police from talking to drivers in the convoys of scab lorries speeding into steelworks 100 at a time, miners have been forced to find other ways of stopping them. There has been a spate of sabotage and attacks on scab lorries and lorry depots in South Wales.

39

Womens support groups grow

Photo: Miners build a barricade to defend themselves against police violence, Orgreave, 18 June 1984 John Sturrock/ Network

The strike has gone way beyond the trade union structure as it has become more and more politicised. It has involved the whole mining community brushing aside deep traditions of prejudice and chauvinism. The women of the mining communities have been the backbone of the strike. Apart from the organisation of welfare and support groups, women have engaged in mass pickets, undertaken country-wide fundraising and speaking tours. So desperate has the state become that a London printer taking food up to Notts mining villages was beaten up by police. Others collecting food and money for the miners have been threatened with arrest, and arrested in some cases, in order to stop support for the strike. The strength of the women has, however, defeated these ploys of the ruling class: they play equal and frequently leading roles in the organisation of the struggle. 'I've seen the change coming for years; but the last few weeks have seen it at its best. If we have arguments at home now, it's about who's going on the picket line and who's going to babysit'. (Miner's wife speaking at Barnsley rally of women's support groups on 12 May 1984).

The miners are also having to learn how to defend themselves against the criminalisation tactics of the police and courts. Day after day they have faced illegal arrests and road blocks, magistrates courts which impose blanket bail conditions, curfews, bindovers and even imprisonment. They have had to learn the hard way that duty solicitors are hand in glove with the police and the magistrates and that they need lawyers who are willing to mount an effective challenge to the courts. The NUM has been painfully slow to provide the legal and political back-up vital if the miners are to defend their democratic rights. For example the police road blocks which have been instrumental in keeping the Notts coalfield working have, as yet, no legal basis. Yorkshire NUM has, at last, after seventeen weeks, begun to challenge the illegal road blocks in the High Court. The opportunity of building a massive campaign against such police tactics has been missed, with damaging consequences for the strike. Some miners have already spent time in prison – and many others will do so. It is vital that they are defended.

It is no coincidence that as the battle between the state and miners has intensified, both sides have increasingly drawn comparisons with Ireland. The NUM newspaper *The Miner* headlined its story of police terror in Notts 'Belfast comes to Blidworth'. Arthur Scargill has said 'the Northern Ireland situation has been brought to the picket lines with the police wearing riot gear'. For the ruling class, the sight of miners building barricades and hurling bricks has raised the spectre of Ireland. After the attack on Kinsley Drift colliery the NCB said it was 'just like Northern Ireland'. A policeman patrolling Shirebrook in North Derbyshire where scabs are being encouraged to return to work said to a reporter: 'I hope this is as close as I ever get to patrolling the streets of Northern Ireland'. Whilst before the strike most miners would have rejected any comparison between their struggle and that of the Irish people, the reality of state repression during the strike is increasingly forcing them to draw the connection. As one miner said to a black *Fight Racism! Fight Imperialism!* comrade: 'We've all got to get together – you, the miners and the Irish, to stop this country in its tracks'.

The Irish connection

13-14 July 1984

Scotland July 1984

In Fife in Scotland 140 children from a local secondary school super-glued their teachers in the staff room, and then marched in procession down to the picket-line with a banner proclaiming 'We support our fathers'. Police stopped them and attempted to turn them back but at that very minute the lorries with coal went past—the children blocked the road and threw paint on to the windscreens, immobilising one lorry.

On another day the coal lorries were routed through the town after breaking the picket and went right past the strike and soup kitchen. When word came to them, the centre full of women, children and some miners on bail conditions, all ran out onto the street to block the lorries. A police jeep drove straight onto the pavement, not striking but knocking to the ground the Chairman of the Strike Committee. Police then leapt out and attacked him, then dragged him semi-conscious into the jeep. A huge fight broke out, with stones and paint flying right into the High Street.

Police riot in Fitzwilliam

On 9 July yet another confrontation took place between police and the community in the mining village of Fitzwilliam, West Yorkshire. Below is an account of the events of Monday 9 July as described to FRFI by the people of Fitzwilliam:

On 9 July, following the continuing police harassment of Brendan Conway, a young miner, the police (who had kept a heavy presence in the village) suddenly attacked people at the local pub, the Fitzwilliam Hotel.

Marching in a 70-strong formation, clad in helmets and with truncheons at the ready. They blocked off the road either side of the pub and then launched an attack on the people in the car park. One bystander, Peter Hurst, was grabbed by 5 police, handcuffed to a post outside the pub and was beaten with truncheons until he was unconscious. His head needed 17 stitches because of his wounds and his blood stains round the car park remained until the next day. Horrified protests from the people to the police were met with 'You can't do anything about it because you have got no witnesses—it's your word against ours!' Peter was then dragged unconscious to the waiting police van. At the same time the police made a bee line for Brendan Conway who was in the pub. He too was handcuffed to a lamp-post and beaten mercilessly with boots and truncheons. He was then thrown into a police van. He needed 5 stitches in his head wounds. Joanne Worth,

for her protests, was assaulted by the police, had her clothes ripped, was smashed in the face with a truncheon and then arrested.

The people stoned the police station and later barricaded off the City estate area. The police refused to enter the area as they were outnumbered and every time they drove near they were stoned by the people. An NCB van and an 'A'-registration car were burned and alarms at the pithead were set off but still the police did not come. Slogans calling for Victory to the Miners were daubed on the walls. Just as in Derry and other nationalist areas of Ireland a no-go area was created. The police eventually re-entered the City estate at 2.30am after people had dispersed. They smashed down Kathleen Doody's door to arrest her son Dennis.

Running battles with the police continued until the early hours of the morning. At one stage the police, and not the miners as has been claimed in the press, closed the main London to Leeds railway to allow 50 riot clad police to march from Hemsworth to Fitzwilliam. At the end of the night 8 people had been arrested, six men and 2 women. They all appeared the next day at a special hearing of the Pontefract Magistrates Court, where they were bailed on the condition that they accepted a curfew from 7.00pm to 7.00am until 21 August when they are due to reappear in court. All 8 have been charged under the Public Order Act with 'breach of the peace'.

JENEFER AND CHAS

42

NEW LESSONS
NEW ALLIES

5

After six months of the miners' strike panic gripped the leaders of the Labour and trade union movement. These staunch upholders of the old order were terrified that their carefully built institutions, based on years of treacherous compromise with the ruling class, would be blown apart if the miners' strike continued outside their control. For the irreconcilable divisions in the NUM and mining communities, between the striking miners and the scabs, were now mirrored throughout the Labour and trade union movement as workers were necessarily forced to take sides. The threat of public exposure of these divisions at the annual Trades Union Congress and Labour Party conferences in September and October only increased the determination of the labour movement leaders to bring Arthur Scargill and the striking miners to heel.

Mass picketing, occupations and sit-ins, barricades, bricks and petrol bombs, sabotage and hit squads have been the miners' response to the state violence and repression launched against their strike. Inevitably the miners, forced to fight in this way against the British imperialist machinery of terror, are identifying their struggle with that of the oppressed who have already taken on the same enemy. For the first time in decades a section of politically conscious workers are identifying their struggle with the revolutionary struggle of the Irish people for freedom. Little wonder that the same Labour and trade union leaders who have fully backed British terror in Ireland and who have ignored the British state's brutal and racist attack on black people, should now be determined to get the miners' strike under their deadly control.

TUC—THE KISS OF JUDAS

The weeks prior to the TUC conference have been marked by unusually hectic activity from trade union leaders devoted to a single end: that of ensuring that Scargill and the NUM do not make a direct appeal to trade unionists over the heads of their leaders. For such an appeal would expose the deep divisions in the conference. The media has faithfully recorded the anxiety and fears of trade union leaders like Murray, Basnett, Duffy, Chapple and Sirs. Talk of the conference 'splitting', of it being 'hijacked' by the miners, of 'chaotic scenes' and even of 'mass violence' from miners inside and outside the conference hall in Brighton, have been used to pressurise the NUM to water down its demands on the TUC. With the prospect of 20,000 miners lobbying the conference Len Murray even took the unprecedented step of meeting with the Chief Constable of Sussex to discuss police tactics – such as whether to use police dogs.

The miners' demands were for simple trade union solidarity: a 10p a week levy from all trade unionists, the declaration that no one should cross a miners' picket line and a ban on the movement of scab coal. These demands, though simple, pose an obvious threat to the unity of a conference whose leaders and members have shown themselves to be deeply divided over support for the miners' cause. The threat of total isolation of the NUM, coming from both 'left' and 'right' trade union leaders, has led to NUM leaders accepting a compromise series of demands. The 10p levy has been dropped and replaced by 'a concerted campaign to raise money . . .'. While trade unionists will be asked not to cross NUM official pickets or use scab coal or fuels, the implementation of this now requires 'detailed discussions with the General Council and agreement with unions who would be directly concerned'. These concessions to reactionary sections of the trade union movement will not advance the miners' position even if they may serve to temporarily paper over the cracks at the conference. On the eve of the conference right-wing trade union leaders are already making it clear that they will take their opposition to the deal into the conference hall. The divisions in the trade union movement are all too real and cannot be papered over, as the second docks strike within two months has shown.

The first docks strike called at the beginning of July, after coal had

been unloaded for BSC at Immingham by non-registered dock labour, soon ended on 23 July after a compromise formula had been agreed and as a result of pressures from dockers in non-registered ports, especially Dover. The second dock strike began on 24 August after BSC's decision to unload coal from the *Ostia* in Hunterston, again using non-registered dock labour, and has demonstrated the deep divisions among dockers in the TGWU. While all twelve dock labour scheme ports in Scotland are on strike and most of those in England and Wales, crucial ports like Dover and Felixstowe are working. The voting at Dover was only 6 out of 488 in favour of a strike. And at Felixstowe where the average wage of 1,532 employees last year was £13,507, only 5 out of 900 supported a strike. A scab branch secretary in Great Yarmouth stated a widely held position of those dockers still working.

The second docks strike

'We have helped the miners in the past with money but we draw a line at this. The talk about scab labour is just an excuse. This is a political strike. We shall work and we shall cross picket lines if we have to.'

Despite the fact that a victory for the miners would be an enormous step forward for the whole working class, the steel workers, power workers and many dockers have chosen to put their narrow sectional interests before those of the working class as a whole. Concessions to such reactionary trade unionists will hold back the future development of a real fighting trade union movement.

STATE VIOLENCE VS WORKERS VIOLENCE

With the breakdown of the last round of talks between the NCB and the miners on 17 July, the NCB has devoted its energies to creating a 'back-to-work' movement in an effort to break the strike. Enormous police operations have been mounted to get scabs through picket lines. 1,000 police were used to get 2 scabs into Gascoigne Wood, Yorkshire, on 17 August. It took five days for police to get one scab, Paul Wilkinson, through barricades and mass pickets into Easington Colliery, Durham on 24 August, and then only by sneaking him in through a back door. Miners responded by throwing bricks, smashing 71 windows of the Easington NCB offices and overturning cars. Police mount round-the-clock guards on scabs' homes and protect meetings organised by scab leaders, such as Chris Butcher (alias Silver Birch) whose activities have been magnified out of all proportion by the NCB and media. In reality the back-to-work movement in solid strike areas was, according to the NCB itself, on 20 August only 160 miners out of 110,000 (0.15 per cent). The NCB has also tried to add to the pressure on striking miners by closing pit faces which they claim are in a dangerous condition and sacking some miners convicted of picketing offences.

Back-to-work movement fails

Far from undermining the strike, these measures and the police-protected 'back-to-work' movement have strengthened the determination of the striking miners. Mass picketing has been stepped up in all areas and miners are finding new forms of resistance to combat the increased violence and intimidation of the police.

Riot police 13 August 1984

Riot police were used for the first time in Nottinghamshire in Warsop on 13 August. Miners and their cars were attacked by police using batons, police cars were driven into miners' cars. Brute force was used to drive pickets out of Warsop three hours before the shift even began. On that day alone, in a small area, police turned back 800 cars in Derbyshire and 600 cars with 3,000 pickets in Notts. On 15 August Scunthorpe, Lincolnshire, was sealed off by 1,000 police who also closed four miles of the A18. Police have launched violent attacks in the Armthorpe area, Yorkshire. One young miner, Adrian Simpson, was put in intensive care in Doncaster Hospital as a result of injuries sustained whilst in police custody. His injuries included a broken jaw, lost teeth, injured arm, broken knuckles and injuries to the back of the head. This is in the same area where on 22 August police sealed off the area and halted bus services. Police in riot gear charged through the village chasing pickets. Local women opened doors to let pickets into safety and police broke down doors, dragged pickets out and beat them. An 84 year old woman was injured. The press were refused entry to the area.

2,000 miners injured

The number of arrests is well over 6,000 and is rising rapidly. One miner has already been sentenced to 9 months in goal. More can be expected as special mobile highly-paid magistrates have been urgently drafted into mining areas. Over 2,000 miners have been injured. It is in response to this level of state violence and police support for the scabs that the striking miners have stepped up their fightback, meeting state violence with workers' violence.

The most striking aspect has been the development of the surprise raids by hit squads of miners doing extensive damage to NCB property and transport. Attacks have included the following: 29 July – an arson attack on the E&J Meeks Transport depot near Mansfield in which nine vehicles were set alight and six completely destroyed. On 5 August – a raid on a transport depot at South Normanton near Mansfield was claimed by an anonymous caller to Radio Nottingham saying he was from the South Nottinghamshire hit squad. He said the raid was part of a campaign against NCB property and the homes of working miners – especially members of the Notts Working Miners Committee. On 7 August – 200 pickets attacked an NCB transport depot and caused £4,000 of damage in 3 minutes, smashing the windows of 15 lorries and a coach. The same night 60 men attacked the Doncaster NCB head-quarters, and 500 men attacked Silverhill colliery, Notts, damaging 18 working miners' cars and smashing all office windows. 1,000 men at Harworth pit smashed windows and attacked cars – 59 were arrested and charged with 'unlawful assembly and threatening behaviour'. Nine police were injured, three seriously. Next day mounted police were used at Harworth and a further 95 were arrested. On 12 August five NCB coaches being fitted with grilles at an engineering works in Notts were totally gutted by fire.

Hit squads emerge

'The people of Ireland and the British miners and the British working class are locked in struggle with the same enemy but on different fronts...

And we have to be honest. As a Labour Movement we often turned our backs, but now we are experiencing the same tactics and we have learnt the lesson, we will remember, and we will stand with all oppressed people against this sort of harassment in the future.' (Malcolm Pitt)

On 15 August Welsh and Notts miners occupied the offices of Price Waterhouse in Birmingham. They are the accountants empowered by the High Court to seize Welsh NUM funds after the NUM had refused to pay a £50,000 fine for contempt of court for picketing scab lorries which were delivering coal to the Port Talbot steel works. More recently South Wales miners have taken direct action to block coal supplies to Welsh steel works. On 30 August they seized a transporter bridge and used it to prevent ships passing up the River Usk, Newport. 80 miners simultaneously occupied a BSC jetty at Port Talbot and climbed onto cranes being used to unload coal. When police surroun-ded the area the miners pelted them with stones and scaffolding poles. Whilst the ruling class and the media have raised a furore about strik-ers' violence they take a different attitude to violence by scabs. On 6 July a scab fired a shot gun out of his house at strikers. The police said this was the right thing to do. Whilst he was not charged, the pickets were.

Scargill has been taunted and beseeched by the media to condemn the miners' violence, but time after time he has refused. Calling the pickets 'magnificent' and saying he took a 'class stand' he said he was not willing, in any circumstances 'to condemn the brave men and women whose only crime is fighting for the right to work'. He received a standing ovation for this from miners' wives at a rally on 11 August. So frustrated is MacGregor at Scargill's principled stand that he suggested on 21 August that Scargill was involved in an 'orchestrated conspiracy'.

'If you have people creating riots somebody has got to be behind that. I believe that in due course the justice of this country should take cognisance of what has been going on. I see evidence of an orchestrated conspiracy...the authorities should examine what the position of Mr Scargill is in this very highly organised orchestration'.

Chapple backs MacGregor

MacGregor received support from the extreme right-wing trade union leader Frank Chapple for his view that there was a conspiracy to create violence in the miners' strike. Chapple stopped short of stating that Scargill should be prosecuted but felt it necessary to state that Scargill was a 'raging egomaniac' and a 'big-headed loud-mouthed bigot'. So much for trade union solidarity.

Kinnock attacks 'violence' again

The attack on workers' violence has not been confined to right-wing trade union leaders and capitalist hatchet men. Labour Party leader Kinnock was eager to dissociate himself from acts of workers' violence, describing them as 'horrific' and 'playing Maggie's game'. 'Violence' he said, 'is no part of British trade unionism'. This is simply a lie. As an historical fact the most militant period of the British working class movement was the time of the Chartist movement in the 1840s. Workers defended themselves against police violence with staves and firearms, they attacked police stations and burned down the houses of those who administered the Poor Law. Similar working class violence was used to defend trade unionism before the First imperialist war. That Kinnock condemns workers' violence is not surprising. He is the leader of a party which has directed state violence against oppressed peoples throughout the world and against black people in Britain.

SWP condemns hit squads

While Kinnock covers up his attack on workers' violence by saying they are playing into the hands of Prime Minister Thatcher, the Socialist Workers Party covers up its attack on miners' hit squads by saying 'such raids can give trade union officials an excuse not to deliver solidarity' (*Socialist Worker* 11 August 1984). In a disgusting attack on miners' resistance through hit squads against attempts by the police, the NCB and scabs to break the strike, they say:

'we are ... opposed to individuals or groups using violence as a substitute for mass struggle. That's why we oppose planting bombs, assassinating politicians and criticise some of the miners' "hit squads".' (*Socialist Worker* 25 August 1984)

Terrified of the revolutionary violence of the oppressed, *Socialist Worker* goes to absurd lengths to tell us that we should only support violence when large numbers are involved. What an unreal world the writers of *Socialist Worker* live in. How else do they think that miners, denied the right to picket and travel, placed on curfew, besieged by police, are to fight back? Nor are these actions divorced from the mass struggle as *Socialist Worker* tries to argue – they obviously complement it.

48

MINERS' RESISTANCE—NEW LESSONS, NEW ALLIES

Three months into the miners' strike we argued that whilst miners were drawing comparisons between the police operation against the miners and that against the nationalist minority in the Six Counties of Ireland and against black people in racist South Africa, they had yet:

'to draw the political conclusion that to defend themselves they must stand in solidarity with these struggles against the British imperialist state'

Only three months later, miners and some of their leaders are now arguing exactly this point. Speaking at a demonstration for British withdrawal from Ireland Malcolm Pitt, President of Kent NUM, stated on 18 August:

'The people of Ireland and the British miners and the British working class are locked in struggle with the same enemy but on different fronts . . .
'And we have to be honest. As a Labour Movement we often turned our backs, but now we are experiencing the same tactics and we have learnt the lesson, we will remember, and we will stand with all oppressed people against this sort of harassment in the future.'

Speaking at an Edinburgh Irish Solidarity Committee meeting protesting against the murder of John Downes by the RUC on Bloody Sunday 12 August 1984 in Belfast, a Fife miner said of his experience at Orgreave:

'It is these such forces the Irish people have fought against for fifteen years and now the miners are faced with similar attacks. When this dispute is won the Irish people must not be left to fight alone.'

Inevitably in such a determined and courageous struggle like that of the miners, former friends are exposed as treacherous enemies as divisions in the working class continue to widen. However, this process is a necessary one. It is laying the basis for rebuilding the working class movement as a fighting force. As old alliances are destroyed by the struggle so are new and more reliable ones formed. It is this aspect of the miners' strike that paves the way for the future – the recognition that British workers have a common interest in uniting with the oppressed everywhere to destroy the common enemy: British imperialism. Real allies of the miners are to be found among the nationalist people fighting for freedom in Ireland, among the black masses fighting against the British-backed apartheid state in South Africa, and among black people fighting the racist British state here in Britain. These developments show that some British trade unionists are at last breaking with the imperialist traditions that have dominated the British Labour and trade union movement since its foundation.

1 September 1984

**Malcolm Pitt—
the miners and
Ireland**

6 STATE AUTHORITY CHALLENGED

A victory for the striking miners was now feared not only by Thatcher and the Tory government but also by the present leadership of the Labour and trade union movement. For such a victory would have been gained through methods of direct confrontation with the state—methods which are totally alien to those who have hung on to their powerful positions in the labour movement through negotiation, compromise and compliance with the ruling class, its laws and institutions. It was the miners' determined resistance to organised police violence and their refusal to comply with the openly political judgements of ruling class courts that took the strike into its eighth month and guaranteed it a lasting political impact on the working class movement in Britain.

Scargill defies High Court

No one more than Arthur Scargill embodies the shift that has taken place in working class politics as a result of the miners' strike. His refusal, for example, to purge his contempt of the High Court judgement of 28 September, which declared that the strike in Yorkshire and Derbyshire was illegal, challenges not only the legitimacy of the courts but also presents a direct political challenge to the likes of Labour Party leader Kinnock and his supporters. Kinnock, ambitious for political power, knows only the path of class compromise and so desperately seeks bourgeois respectability. For him the law is above class conflict. So he rebukes us with the warning that 'we cannot . . . scorn legality because it does not suit us at the present time'. In contrast Arthur Scargill states that he would rather go to prison than betray his class: 'I stand by my class, by my union – and if that means prison so be it. We have come too far, we have suffered too much for there to be any compromise with either the judiciary or the government'. Scargill and Kinnock represent the fundamentally divergent paths which now face the British working class as a result of the miners' strike. In this way the miners' strike has dramatically demonstrated that divisions are a necessary precondition not only for the victory of the miners' strike but for the political advance of the working class as a whole.

TUC CONFERENCE

The 1984 TUC Conference (3-7 September) took place amidst speculation that it would be the scene of a major battle over support for the

50

striking miners. As miners fought police on the picket lines at pits throughout the country the TUC, as expected, passed a resolution which was designed to promise everything and deliver nothing. The resolution, couched in deliberately vague terms, supported the NUM's opposition to pit closures, pledged a 'concerted campaign' to raise money, and asked members not to move coal or coke or oil substituted for coal or coke across NUM official picket lines, and not to use oil substituted for coal – the latter two points to be subject to full discussion with the TUC General Council and relevant unions. The motion was overwhelmingly passed. The General Council had achieved its objective of temporarily papering over the potential cracks and divisions in the TUC caused by the miners' strike. There were no riots outside the Conference Hall – only 4-5,000 gathered outside. There were no battles on the Congress floor. The scabs, led by Eric Hammond (Electrical Electronic Telecommunications and Plumbing Union – EETPU), made an ineffective appearance and were booed. The Amalgamated Union of Engineering Workers (AUEW) could now 'support' the miners as they had been drawn back into the TUC fold. Len Murray, retiring TUC General Secretary, all too clearly explained the aim of the whole exercise when he said that 'the purpose of the procedures set out in the statement is to devise arrangements to make the dispute more effective and to make mass picketing unnecessary'. He also used his speech to attack 'picket line violence'. 'There have been scenes which reflect no credit whatsoever on the standing and reputation of the trade union movement'. The very next day, the conference gave a standing ovation to Kinnock, 'the policemen's friend', when he, too, attacked the miners' fightback against police violence:

TUC resolution

Photo: Scargill stands by his class
Chris Davies/ Network

'violence, I do not have to tell this Congress... disgusts union opinion and divides union attitudes...and is alien to the temperament and the intelligence of the British trade union movement'.

As we accurately pointed out on the eve of conference, even the paper-thin unity achieved by this resolution has barely resulted in a shred of increased support for the miners. The cracks began to show even as the conference ended. Terry Duffy, leader of the AUEW, confided to *The Observer* (9 September 1984) at the end of the

51

conference: 'There's no way our members are going to support any shutdown of a power station.'

The Economist (8 September 1984), voice of the industrial bourgeoisie, cynically summed up the whole miserable affair.

'The fudge which will end Britain's six-month-old coal strike is already clear . . . It is now unlikely that the vehicle of this defeat will be either Mrs Thatcher or Mr MacGregor . . . on Monday the Trades Union Congress took the first shambling step, six months late, towards this defeat when its moderate executive gathered the miners into the bear-hug of "total support" – support which it has neither the capacity nor the intention to deliver.'

Following the conference, TUC leaders sought to wring every possible concession from the NUM and to place every obstacle in the way of gaining support. On 16 September it was reported that 'senior' TUC leaders were making support contingent on the NUM being seen to do everything in their power to get a settlement, insisting for example that the NUM go to see the Advisory Conciliation and Arbitration Service (ACAS).

Second docks strike ends

The miners continue to receive financial and material assistance from a wide cross-section of the working class. But still no real effective solidarity action which would decisively affect the outcome of the strike has taken place. The second docks strike to take place during the miners' strike was never total, and was restricted throughout mainly to ports covered by the dock labour scheme. The end of the strike on 19 September was brought about by an agreement between dockers and steel workers unions for quotas of coal going into Ravenscraig which actually rise *above* those agreed before. 18,000 tons per week are to be allowed in for the first month, 20,000 for the second, then 22,500 the month after. Instrumental in this shameful agreement, which completely turned its back on the miners' needs, were the Labour Party Shadow Transport spokesman John Prescott and Labour MP for Motherwell South, Jeremy Bray. The deal was roundly condemned by Arthur Scargill who said 'The NUM do not expect anyone to make deals which result in people crossing our picket lines'.

The workers in the power industry remain bitterly divided over the possibility of action in support of the miners. After a meeting of the nine unions involved on 28 September, the general unions – the TGWU and the General Municipal Boilermakers and Allied Trades Union (GMBATU) – said they would ask their members to take action. Others, particularly the main crafts unions – the EETPU (Eric Hammond) and the Engineers and Managers Association EMA (John Lyons) – strongly opposed any blocking of coal.

On the railways, despite action by a number of workers, coal continues to be moved from the working Notts coalfield. The threatened NUR/ASLEF action in September against rail cuts was withdrawn so that further talks could take place. No doubt British Rail was told by Thatcher, as happened earlier in the miners' strike, to run no risk of a rail strike at the present time. Support from power and rail workers will become absolutely vital if the government begins the attempt to move pit-head coal stocks – as is widely suggested must happen during November if power cuts are to be avoided.

THE LABOUR PARTY CONFERENCE

At the TUC Conference the dead weight of the TUC leadership was able to effectively tone down the impact of the miners' strike on its proceedings. At the Labour Party Conference, however, this was not possible to anything like the same degree. First, many Labour Party activists were present who are involved in miners' support groups and who have had direct experience of police harassment and arrest when collecting food and money for the miners. Second, High Court writs were served on Arthur Scargill and four other NUM leaders on the first day of the conference, threatening massive fines and a possible gaol sentence for contempt of court because they continue to insist that the strike in Yorkshire and Derbyshire remains official. The refusal of the miners' leaders to comply with the writ, the unanimous decision of the NUM Executive to back Arthur Scargill in stating that the strike remained official and the presence of the miners' leader in the conference hall on Thursday at the time he was due to appear in the High Court ensured that the miners' strike remained the central issue of the Labour Party Conference. Kinnock's major speech to the conference in which he equated workers' violence with state violence and argued that the law had to be obeyed come what may was totally eclipsed by the miners' principled stand. Kinnock's slavish adherence to ruling class law was effectively neutralised by this example of real class politics.

Photo: Kinnock scabs on miners throughout the strike
Mike Abrahams/
Network

The prelude to the Labour Party Conference in the week beginning 1 October was marked by a series of manoeuvres which vainly attempted to limit the effect of the miners' strike on the conference and in particular to eliminate from the conference agenda any criticism of police violence against the miners. This, above all, was the issue which could acutely embarrass Neil Kinnock and be a setback for his ambitions of being a future Prime Minister. Despite press rumours of some back stage deal struck between Kinnock, Orme and Scargill (rumours which Scargill vigorously denied) the NUM resolution attacking police violence went forward to the conference. In addition, a section of the NEC statement to conference on the miners' strike which criticised pickets' violence, was deleted. In the event, Scargill received two standing ovations and four motions were passed which criticised police behaviour. In his speech Scargill said 'Yes we've got violence – state violence against the miners'.

Throughout the week prior to the Labour Party Conference endless challenges were thrown down to Kinnock to condemn 'picket line violence'. Kinnock was faced with a choice: either to make a concession to Thatcher, or to make a concession to the miners. Pressure at the Labour Party Conference in fact forced Kinnock to give the 'left' version of his argument against miners' violence in his major conference speech. 'I condemn *all* violence' he said ' . . . the violence of the stone throwers and the battering ram carriers' (the miners) '*and* the shield bangers and cavalry chargers' (the police). Kinnock 'abhors' violence, he tells us; he wants nothing to do with it. However, he only uses this 'neutral' position as a stick to beat the miners. He is soon back into a familiar theme of the police being the 'meat in the sandwich' – between Thatcher and the miners. While Thatcher stands for her class – the ruling class – Kinnock sits on the fence and betrays the working class. Unlike Scargill, whose very experience has told him that the police are a special body of armed men who exist solely to protect the interests of the capitalist state, Kinnock has shown that he has much more to fear from the revolutionary violence of the oppressed than from the batons of the riot police.

Kinnock's speech then proceeded to the question of legality: 'democracy is the socialist's only way and route to power. We cannot sharpen legality as our main weapon for the future and then simultaneously scorn legality because it does not suit us at the present time'. This is just pure deception. As Kinnock well knows, *any* defence of trade union rights at the present time involves breaking the law. Without breaking the law, the miners would have been defeated months ago. Kinnock wants nothing to do with militant trade unionism. A TGWU attempt to put a motion to the conference openly siding with the NUM's defiance of the High Court was dropped lest the Labour Party and trade union leaders should – horror of horrors – be found to be in contempt of the law themselves.

Following the Labour Party Conference criticism of police violence against the miners, Police Federation chairman, Leslie Curtis, made it clear that the police might be unable to serve the public under a future Labour government. In what he called a 'warning shot' to the Labour leaders, Curtis demonstrated the police's contempt for democracy, and showed the conscious political role that the police intend to play in future events. That his statement was backed by Home Secretary Leon Brittan shows the true contempt that the ruling class has for legality and democracy if it ceases to work in its favour.

STATE ORCHESTRATED VIOLENCE

The government and the NCB have strained every nerve to get the 'back-to-work' movement off the ground in striking areas. On 28 September Thatcher personally visited police stationed at the North York-

54

At Labour Party Conference, Kinnock 'abhors' all violence

Police Federation 'warns' Labour Party

shire division police headquarters and, in the manner of a general addressing her troops, told police who had just returned from duty at Kellingley colliery that she was 'extremely grateful' for what they were doing. As the police have more and more been confronted by the striking miners' refusal to be beaten, they have had to raise the spectre of new and evil forces at work, in order to justify their increasingly brutal role. The argument often takes opposing forms, ranging from describing picketing as being 'master-minded' violence, to being the product of some lunatic element. Leslie Curtis, Police Federation chairman, has accused the NUM of:

> 'a sustained campaign of out-and-out lawlessness which is without precedent in this country ... It is even worse than the inner city riots of 1981 because they were not planned or masterminded, and the police were able to restore order and normality quickly ... '

Eldon Griffiths, Tory MP who speaks for the police, stated 'police will soon need to be equipped with plastic bullets to combat armed pickets firing airguns and other weapons'. On 28 September the so-called 'ambush' took place of 20 police in *nine* dog vans and a landrover near Silverwood pit, where the main injuries to police appear to have been caused by bites from their own dogs. Eldon Griffiths stated that this was 'a further and deadly serious escalation of the criminal violence being employed by lunatic or drunken fringes of Mr Scargill's private army ... There is all the difference in the world between the illegal violence of the pickets which strikes at the very heart of civil liberty and parliamentary democracy and the use by police of the lawful force they are required to use to uphold the Queen's Law.'

Photo: Picketer beaten by riot police, Maltby, Yorkshire, 24 September 1984 John Sturrock/ Network

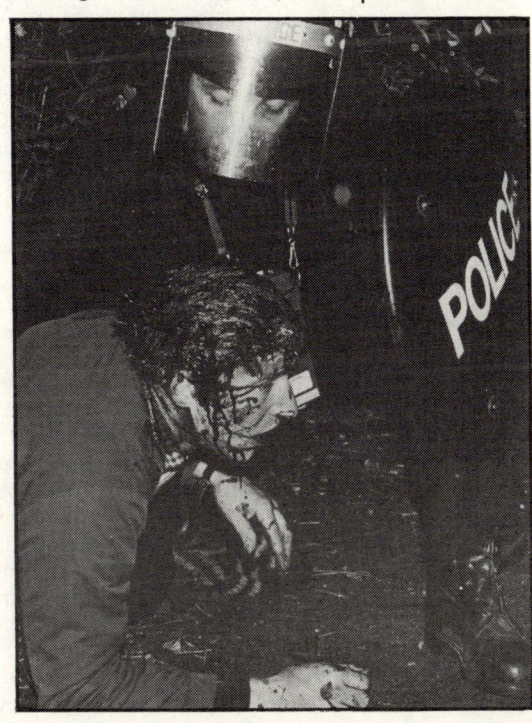

What these 'outraged' statements are laying the basis for is the now daily reality of policing on the picket lines. Not just once or twice, but day in, day out, riot police, horses and dogs are now used in an attempt to open up the striking pits and break the strikers' resistance. Over two weeks alone, the police operation to get seven scabs into Kiveton Park colliery cost £350,000, according to the local parish council. Arrests on 2 October stood at 7,149. 39 miners had been sent to gaol and curfews up to 24 hours continue to be imposed. In a threatening speech,

Home Secretary Leon Brittan stated, referring to those charged with so-called 'intimidation' of scabs:

'Some of those are charged with serious offences carrying very severe maximum penalties . . . Those tempted to try their hand at violence and crime in future might care to reflect on the fact that arson, assault causing grievous bodily harm and criminal damage with intent to endanger life, are offences which carry life sentences as a maximum.'

He added that serious criminal damage carries a prison sentence of up to 10 years and that there were 'no limits' to charges for riot and affray. Since pickets are arrested on any pretext this means that *any* miner deciding to picket runs the risk of a long prison sentence. Seven miners have been charged under the Conspiracy and Protection of Property Act of 1875 which was last used against the Shrewsbury building workers – three of whom were sent to prison. Four miners have now been arrested for allegedly shouting 'death-threats' at Robert Taylor as he was driving in his car. Taylor is one of the miners from Manton colliery who had the writ served on Arthur Scargill. Three of the four miners charged have been remanded in custody. It isn't difficult to imagine the sort of justice that will be handed out after a press campaign of lies and slander against them.

A *Panorama* programme during this period showed the part that the NCB plays in this operation. An NCB manager could be seen in his office at Warsop colliery with detailed wall maps showing every working and striking miner's house marked in different colours. Each potential 'scab' was discussed in detail by the managers and was later visited by NCB representatives. The 'back-to-work' movement is an organised conspiracy of NCB officials and the police against the NUM. A miner at Barnburgh pit near Doncaster recently admitted that he had gone back to work for a day. He had only made a casual enquiry to his pit manager when the police phoned him up several weeks later to say that arrangements had been made to escort him into work. When he began to object he was told that thousands of pounds had been spent on arrangements, so he eventually went along with them. He could only stomach one day.

MINERS' RESISTANCE

Back-to-work movement fails again

The much-heralded 'back-to-work' day to coincide with the TUC Conference debate on the miners on 3 September failed to materialise. Since then in nearly every area massive battles have been provoked by police trying to get handfuls of scabs into pits. On 3 September 26 miners reported for work at Tilmanstone in Kent. The return was militantly resisted by pickets, ranged against hundreds of police, many from London. 30 arrests were made, including Malcolm Pitt, Kent NUM President. On that night, police prevented people in the nearby village of Elvington from leaving their homes after 8.30pm. The following day another 20 miners were arrested. Jack Collins, Kent NUM Secretary stated: 'There is a conspiracy against the miners by the police, the magistrates, the law courts, the bloody lot.' On 5 September, the Kent miners fought back. At Betteshanger colliery 12 police were hurt, at Tilmanstone straw fires were started and trees felled to make barricades. The return to work in Kent has been halted.

At the Yorkshire pits situated on the largest coalfields decisive battles are being fought by miners resisting riot-clad and mounted police attacks. Kellingley, North Yorkshire, is the biggest pit in Britain and so would be a vital component in breaking the strike. On 6 September 4,000 pickets gathered to stop two scabs. Police carrying long riot shields moved against pickets – one of whom was taken unconscious to hospital. An ITN camera crew's car was overturned and set on fire. The A645 was closed for two hours. Police attacks at Kellingley carried on for five days.

Kellingley

At Kiveton Park, near Sheffield, on 7 September hundreds of riot police chased pickets through streets and gardens. 3,000 pickets had arrived in the early hours of the morning to find mounted riot police in wait. Roads were sealed off and police used searchlights to try and pick out leaders. As the scabs arrived in their armoured van, police wielded long staves against pickets, batoning them to the ground and chasing them over walls. Those arrested had their hands bound behind their backs with strips of leather. This has only strengthened the resolve of the striking miners. Mass picketing has continued ever since.

Kiveton Park

At Maltby pit on 21 September, 6,000 pickets arrived to stop 7 construction workers from going in to work. It can be no coincidence at all that the construction company involved is none other than Cementation Ltd, builder of universities in Oman, employer of the services of Mark Thatcher, owned by close pal of Thatcher, Nigel Broackes. Police in riot gear battled the next day with 4,500 pickets. Armoured vans with shields attached were used to shelter riot police as they charged the picket lines. MP Kevin Barron, who tried to stop pickets throwing stones and got struck by police batons for his pains said that the men who attacked him were wearing boiler suits without numbers. A young miner, Ian Wright, was batoned to the ground and kicked unconscious. Pickets stated that the police behaved 'like animals'.

Maltby

On 1 October one of the biggest police operations of the seven-months strike took place at Manton colliery, Notts, to get four scabs into work including Robert Taylor and Ken Foulstone – the two miners who want to put Arthur Scargill in gaol. A vast army of police using helicopter surveillance, horses and dogs, were used to prevent picketing miners blocking their return to work.

Manton

This militant response to each and every attempt to break the strike continues and has prevented any 'back-to-work' movement from emerging in the militant areas. According to NCB figures at the end of September, in Yorkshire only 40 out of 54,000 miners have gone back; in Kent 30 out of 2,300; in South Wales none out of 24,000; only five pit workers and ten white collar workers in the North East; and 300 out of 13,000 in Scotland. The only area where the NCB has had any more than a negligible success is North Derbyshire where 20 to 30 miners are going back to work each week as a result of an intensive campaign by the NCB and police. By the end of September according to the NCB, 1,000 out of

NATIONAL UNION OF MINEWORKERS

DIG DEEP FOR THE Miners

10,000 miners in North Derbyshire had gone back – well below the expected figure planned hoped for by the NCB.

MINERS STRIKE AT THE CROSSROADS?

According to a whole number of sources, coal stocks will be at a critical level of around eight million tons by November. The latest survey by a firm of City stockbrokers estimates that there is 4-6 million tons at the working pits, with three million tons stockpiled in Holland. Coal imports have doubled since July last year – to £20.7 million from £10.9 million (mostly from the US, Poland and the EEC) and oil imports have increased 2½ times – to £141.6 million from £63.6 million last year. Oil is 50% more expensive to use than coal in the production of electricity. £750 million has been added on to the cost of electricity since the beginning of the miners' strike and the government is now considering the imposition of a 'Scargill levy' on electricity bills. All of this means that the government, if power cuts are to be avoided, is more and more faced with the prospect of having to move the 18 million tons of coal still stored at strike bound pit heads. To move this coal would almost definitely involve the use of troops and would bring massive confrontations with miners and possibly other sections of the labour movement. It is for this reason that the 'back-to-work' movement option has been played so vigorously during the last month. Unless the major pits in Yorkshire and other areas are now opened up, Thatcher will have no choice but to up the confrontation stakes or to accept defeat.

On the first day of the TUC Conference, half-an-hour before the debate on the miners began, new talks were announced between the NCB and NUM. For the rest of the week they were on and then off. Finally the talks began on 8 September, and broke down five days later over the fundamental issue of 'uneconomic' pits. The NUM has unwaveringly refused to accept MacGregor's definition of 'economic' as one that is simply geared to profits – one which leaves on one side the devastation and waste of whole communities and future generations. As Arthur Scargill has pointed out, 81% of new investment has been in the central coalfields as opposed to those of Scotland and South Wales, where many of the pits have, as a result, been designated 'uneconomic'. For these reasons the NUM refused to accept MacGregor's latest pathetic attempt to gloss over the issue. The NCB's new terms were that they must retain the right to decide the future of pits 'in line with their responsibilities'. As is well known by now, MacGregor's 'responsibilities' are solely to the brutal logic of capitalism and to Thatcher's aim of crushing the NUM.

NACODS vote for strike

On Friday 28 September the result was declared in the strike ballot of the 17,000 strong pit deputies union – the National Association of Colliery Overseers Deputies and Shotfirers (NACODS). The 82.5% majority was in favour of strike action over the decision on 15 August by the NCB to stop the pay of deputies who refused to cross picket

58

lines, and in opposition to pit closures and the breakdown of conciliation procedures. This significant display of support for the NUM's aims
was followed by further talks between NACODS and the NCB in order
to prevent the total shutdown of all pits, including the working pits,
should NACODS decide to take strike action. The NCB is considering
the NACODS' proposal that an independent arbitrator should decide
on pit closures. The NCB has submitted counter-proposals to ACAS
and are to meet NACODS again on Sunday 7 October. The NUM also
met ACAS on Saturday 6 October. Pressure is inevitably building up on
the NCB and government as the autumn days draw in and coal stocks
are run down. No doubt we shall also see increased pressure from
Labour and trade union leaders on the NUM to force it into some form
of unprincipled compromise.

On Wednesday 10 October Arthur Scargill and the NUM will face a
second contempt of court allegation when the adjourned case against
them resumes in court. Scargill has said that he is fully prepared to go to
gaol and has repeatedly defied the court by stating that the strike is
official and that the NUM retains the right to discipline any miners
crossing picket lines. On Thursday 4 October the High Court backed
down 'giving time for reflection' and adjourned the case. It cannot do
this again without losing credibility. A decisive test of strength must
soon take place.

A FIGHTING WORKING CLASS MOVEMENT

Every day that the miners' strike continues new lessons are learned. Old
allies are exposed as treacherous enemies and new allies are found
amongst forces that had previously been disregarded. A victory for the
striking miners would fundamentally alter the character of the working
class movement in Britain. For the striking miners will only have won
through direct confrontation with the capitalist state, its police, courts
and laws. A miners' victory would represent a defeat for the Kinnocks,
the Murrays and a whole generation of opportunists who have controlled and held back the struggle of the working class for decades. A whole
layer of militant and victorious miners and their supporters will have
learnt to reject the cringing subservience to bourgeois 'legality' and
bourgeois 'democracy' that is the hallmark of these opportunists.

Because the striking miners have had to politically confront the
divisions in their own ranks, they can understand the significance of
political divisions within the working class movement itself. They now
understand that when the likes of Kinnock or Murray speak of 'unity',
it is a 'unity' that is ultimately only in the interests of the ruling class
itself. Yes, the miners' strike has deepened the divisions in the working
class but only to demonstrate that such divisions are necessary for the
political advance of the working class as a whole. The miners' strike
places on the agenda the rebuilding of the working class movement on a
fighting basis. The next few weeks will provide a decisive test for the
miners and their leaders whose courage and determination have already
transformed the political experience of thousands of people.

5-6 October 1984

7 FIGHT TO THE FINISH

The blazing barricades lit by the 5,000 strong mass picket at Cortonwood on 9 November signalled the determination of the striking miners to halt the latest 'back-to-work' movement and to regain once again the initiative in the power struggle between the NUM and the Thatcher government. Five mass rallies were called by the NUM Executive in key areas to prepare the striking miners for a fight to the finish, as well as to counteract what Arthur Scargill called the 'vile propaganda of the media against the strike'. 3,000 attended a mass rally in Edinburgh on 6 November. And significantly the battle of Cortonwood took place the morning after the mass rally in nearby Sheffield. 4,000 miners, their families and supporters crammed into Sheffield City Hall with an additional two thousand in overflow halls. They heard Peter Heathfield, General Secretary of the NUM urge them to 'stand firm, remain united and together we can weather the storm'. By Monday 12 November, barricades had appeared throughout South Yorkshire and the miners were defending themselves against police with stones, bricks and petrol bombs.

The miners' strike is in a critical phase. A whole series of NCB/government measures over the last few weeks have been deliberately designed to exert maximum pressure on striking miners and their families. The breaking off of two sets of negotiations, the settling of the pit deputies' (NACODS) threatened strike, the offering of huge pay packets to encourage scabbing, the sacking of hundreds of miners who have been convicted in the courts, a series of High Court attacks on NUM funds – have all been coordinated at the highest level by the NCB and government in an effort to demoralise and weaken the strike.

LABOUR LEADERS ATTACK NUM

But the pressure on the strikers has not only come from the NCB and the government. At crucial moments throughout the strike the leadership of the TUC and Labour Party has intervened in order to force the NUM into an unprincipled compromise and, in particular, to undermine the position of Arthur Scargill.

60

At the end of October major disputes in the NCB were beginning to surface and be made public. MacGregor's handling of the strike was being seriously questioned inside the NCB itself. A rapid series of MacGregor-style promotions and demotions took place among top NCB managers. However a story in the *Sunday Times* on an NUM Libyan connection came to the rescue and was promoted to divert attention from what even the British Association of Colliery Management (BACM) called 'incompetence at the highest level' in the NCB. Foremost among the NUM's critics were none other than the General Secretary of the TUC, Norman Willis, and the leader of the Labour Party, Kinnock.

Splits in the NCB

The NUM chief executive Roger Windsor was invited by Libyan trade unionists to visit Libya. Windsor's visit was sensationalised in the media and the subject of an orgy of criticism – led off by Willis and Kinnock. Without asking the NUM for a word of explanation, Willis stated publicly 'I have expressed to Mr Scargill my condemnation of the meeting with Colonel Gadafy. This has created the impression that the NUM is prepared to consort with a government which is heavily implicated in terrorist campaigns outside its own borders.' Mr Willis has no difficulty at all on the other hand, about keeping quiet about the murder of children and innocent people by plastic bullets fired by *British* soldiers and the RUC in the *British*-occupied Six Counties of Ireland.

Willis and Kinnock attack NUM over Libya

Kinnock, too, rushed to pontificate: 'Any offers from them (the Libyans)...would be an insult to everything the British trade union movement stands for. If such offers are ever made, then of course they must and will be rejected.' Kinnock, who has not lifted a finger to help the miners, who has actively scabbed on the miners all the way through and who is not prepared to attend a single one of the five mass NUM rallies, using the lame excuse that his diary is 'too full', still thinks he has the right to dictate from which countries the NUM may receive aid. In fact the NUM is receiving help from trade unionists in fifty countries. During October, a ship of food from Denmark, the Soviet Union and socialist countries, and one from France, arrived to bring food and other goods to support the miners and their families. Such international solidarity is in stark contrast to the actions of those scab leaders of the British labour movement, Kinnock and Willis, who chose to attack the NUM over the Libyan visit while remaining silent over the seizure of NUM funds by ruling class courts in the same week.

During October the TUC attempted to exert more and more control over the strike, even at one point negotiating at ACAS with the pit deputies' union NACODS and the NCB, while Scargill and the NUM were left waiting out in the cold. Jack Eccles, new TUC chairman, celebrated his appointment by attacking the NUM, talking of the 'rigidity of our colleagues in the NUM' and stating that it was time for them to seriously consider the NCB's terms. On the very day that pickets fought riot police at Cortonwood for several hours, this spineless nonentity, Eccles, announced that he doesn't believe 'that the miners' union can achieve its aims of a 100 per cent victory over the Coal Board'. These opportunists, the likes of Willis, Eccles and

'There are a lot of miners who have been picked up and locked up in prison today and if I have one criticism of the NUM ... it's this: they have not yet thought out clearly their position in relation to their imprisoned comrades and that is a grave weakness ... Will they be forgotten about or is it just a memory, a demonstration outside the prisons now and again? How are their comrades to behave when they are locked in prison? ... If they are political prisoners obviously they must then fight for political status within the prison, that is something that the miners, as far as I know, haven't yet thought about. We in occupied Ireland ... learned that lesson late but neverthless we learned it from experience; we had to fight for political status and political prisoners in this country, although they are not recognised as political prisoners, have nevertheless achieved quite a lot over the last ten years ... struggling on different fronts, trying to educate different prisoners around us, struggling against horrible conditions and paying a fairly heavy penalty for that struggle ... '

JOHN McCLUSKEY, IRISH SOLIDARITY MOVEMENT WEEKEND 13/14 OCTOBER 1984

Kinnock, represent the barrier which lies between the striking miners and a victory over the Thatcher government and the NCB. Without their leadership of the working class the Thatcher government and the NCB could not have stood its ground.

Solidarity action in the British trade union movement of the type that would bring about a speedy resolution of the dispute, has remained at a low level. The majority of those workers who are crucial if the strike is to succeed, are not prepared to put the interests of the miners and the working class as a whole, above their own immediate interests. The leadership of these unions reinforces this narrow, sectional outlook.

The calling of a strike by the pit deputies union NACODS, after their ballot of 82.5% in favour of strike action struck terror into the government. The mere prospect of such a strike, coupled with a fall in the price of British oil, led to the biggest fall ever in one day of the *Financial Times* 30 share index – a fall of 27.9 points. £3.7 billion was wiped off share prices in one day. This is why, in the talks arranged at ACAS prior to the strike date, the NCB was obviously instructed to reach an agreement with the pit deputies. To clinch matters, TUC leaders Willis, Basnett and Buckton were called into the negotiations and on 24 October, the eve of the proposed strike, the strike was called off after the NCB had gone some way to meeting NACODS' demands. The TUC leaders were just as eager as Thatcher and Mac-Gregor to get the strike called off. A complete shutdown of the coalfields would have necessitated the use of troops to move coal from strikebound pit heads. This would have entailed a degree of confrontation which the TUC would have had no hope of controlling. As a result of the strike being called off, pit deputies are still being picketed out in many areas, and safety cover withdrawn.

In another key area, the power

stations, only certain sections of workers have been prepared to come to the aid of the miners. The power workers' union, the EETPU, whose leader Eric Hammond has been most vociferous of all in his condemnation of the miners, voted in a secret ballot by 84% (of a 54% turnout) not to back the TUC guidelines in support of the miners. It was hard to imagine how much further Hammond, the bosses' friend, would go until he announced on 8 November that his plan for his union to apply for membership of the Confederation of British Industry 'was not a joke'. Not satisfied with selling out workers' interests to the bosses he now wants to be part of them.

Hammond wants to join CBI

On the other hand, manual workers in the TGWU at Yorkshire power stations have voted not to handle coal or oil. As a result the Central Electricity Generating Board has reduced their share of the national grid from 33% to 4%. In the Trent Valley power stations, purposely situated near the 'moderate' Notts coalfields, and which produce 33% of the national grid, manual workers at only one power station, West Burton, agreed to block coal and oil, but backed down after management pressure. An important development has been the decision by transport and engineering unions at West Thurrock power station in Essex to block the delivery of oil supplies. This has now been taken out of the national grid. Shop stewards at Tilbury power station

Photo: Burning barricades to stop police charges
Geoff Morley

63

had voted to block oil supplies. Moves are also afoot with international trade unions to coordinate a total ban on coal imports.

CLASS WAR—RULING CLASS STRATEGY

The degree of planning and cooperation between the government and MacGregor, becomes more apparent each day. Geoffrey Kirk, Director of Information at the NCB, who has just resigned after being sent on leave by MacGregor without a word of explanation, appeared on TV on 6 November. He said he had been 'rather surprised' to discover that Mrs Thatcher's personal adviser from the advertising company Saatchi and Saatchi, was also advising MacGregor on the conduct of the miners' strike. There can be no doubt now that Thatcher is prepared to risk everything and spend anything in the defeat of Arthur Scargill and the NUM. Fifty per cent of electricity is now being produced by burning oil – the most expensive method possible – at a probable net extra cost of £15 million per week. Leon Brittan announced at the Tory Party Conference unlimited funding for local authorities (over and above that raised on ¾ of a penny rate) for the policing of the miners' strike. Chairman of the Confederation of British Industry Sir Terence Beckett, has stated that 'firms would be prepared to suffer cutbacks and closure to help to defeat Mr Scargill'. The Tories and the ruling class are in no doubt that the class war is on.

Brittan offers unlimited funding to police

In a highly coordinated fashion, a whole number of tactics have been deployed against the miners. Since 7 October, two protracted sets of negotiations involving ACAS have taken place and broken down. These cat-and-mouse negotiations have not only succeeded in tying up NUM leaders for days on end, but have been cruelly used to raise and then dash the hopes of striking miners and their families. The first set of negotiations between the NUM and the NCB at ACAS, lasted for four days and ended on 15 October. Scargill stated that the NCB maintained its insistence on pit closures on economic grounds without consultation. Throughout the negotiations, NCB officials telephoned government departments for briefings. The second set of negotiations took place in the aftermath of the settlement of the NACODS strike threat. The government stated immediately after this that no more was on offer for the NUM and, after twenty more hours of negotiation, this was shown to be the case. The government has now announced that *no* negotiated settlement is possible.

MacGregor and Amax

Along with the on/off negotiations, a whole number of brutal strike-breaking measures have been brought in by MacGregor, no doubt tried and tested in his days as head of the American mining conglomerate Amax which did business with, among others, South Africa and Namibia. From 1967-77 MacGregor was chief executive and chairman and during that time took the company into coal mining in the US. The company took over strip mines in the Western area which were unionised by the United Mineworkers of America. MacGregor made it his business to break the grip of the union which he eventually achieved after a long and bitter struggle. Now 60% of American coal is produced by non-union labour. Only 25% of miners in the Western

64

area are unionised. There is no doubt that it is this aspect of MacGregor's ability which is so attractive to Thatcher and persuaded her to pay over £1 million to borrow him from the merchant bank Lazard Frères.

One of MacGregor's vile tactics is the sacking of miners convicted of offences concerning theft or damage to NCB property. 330 men had been sacked by 20 October. In Yorkshire, 85 have been sacked including fifteen from Grimethorpe and thirty from Rossington in connection with coal picking. This activity used to be allowed during coal disputes but now it has become an offence. Miners' families are not only being starved by denial of full DHSS benefits, but are now being sacked if they are caught gathering tiny amounts of coal to stop their families going cold. The incident at Grimethorpe where riot police with truncheons attacked twenty-two people picking coal from a tip, ignited the fury of the community. On 15 October they smashed every window in the local police station, overturned a police car and attacked two police officers. Miners in Grimethorpe and elsewhere have made it clear that coal which they have produced with their own labour belongs to them. In North Derbyshire where the NCB is waging a vicious propaganda war to try and get the back-to-work movement going, more than 100 miners have been sacked. As Gordon Butler, NUM Secretary for Derbyshire said 'We shall put reinstatement at the top of any agenda and the lads won't go back without them.'

Punitive measures are also being used to try and prevent solidarity action for the miners. Railway workers refusing to transport coal at the big Coalville depot in Leicestershire are being sent home without pay. Managers are threatening to close down the whole depot. In addition, railway police visits to the homes of a number of Coalville railmen who have supported the miners, have resulted in the

Malcolm Pitt is President of Kent NUM and early in the miners' strike was imprisoned for his refusal to accept bail conditions restricting his activity. On the day of the ISM Conference 800 French trade unionists had arrived in Kent with 400 tons of food and £58,000. Malcolm Pitt nevertheless came to the conference and took his stand on the side of the Irish people.

'And we hear, too, all the arguments about ballots, about votes, about the process of democracy. We do not concede that any person has the right to put a cross on a piece of paper to vote somebody else out of a job. We will not concede that these people in government have a right to lecture the NUM and also the British Labour and trade union movement on the virtues of democracy. These people ... have no right to lecture the British miners ... because these are the people who have denied the Irish people the right to unity and nationhood. These are the people who for years played the Orange card and gerrymandered the constituencies of Derry and Belfast. And these are the people who for over 200 years have kept half the people of the world in the chains of imperialist oppression with their armies and their thugs.'

charging of three men with the theft of £4 worth of British Rail property. For this they have been sacked.

The desperation of the ruling class in the face of the determined fight-back of the miners has led to a new twist to ruling class propaganda. After the IRA bomb at Brighton, Thatcher took further the comparison of miners' pickets with so-called 'terrorism' by linking the miners directly with the IRA. She stated that 'the nation now faces the most testing crisis of our time – the battle between the extremists and the rest'. Adam Butler, a junior defence minister, in attacking the striking miners made it clear after Cortonwood that the IRA is not the only threat from within. Such propaganda will totally backfire as miners themselves are comparing their own struggle against the British state with that of the nationalist communities in the Six Counties.

CLASS WAR–PICKETS VS POLICE

'Our police force, whether on the mainland or northern Ireland, has already been deploying tactics which I do not believe have any part in a democratic society... It is high time this or any other government recognised what they are doing now is using the police as a strategic arm of the state machine to batter trade unionists into submission.' (Arthur Scargill on Scottish Radio)

Mass pickets have occurred almost daily in Yorkshire where major battles have taken place against the police. Pickets have heroically resisted mounted riot police, armoured vans driven at speed, dogs and baton charges in an attempt to prevent scabs going into work. At Woolley colliery, West Yorkshire, on 15 October, 25 police were injured; on 30 October the Woolley NUM Branch Secretary went to complain about dogs being set on pickets and was smashed on the side of the head with truncheons. His son was arrested for helping him up from the ground. On 2 November at Woolley, police indiscriminately inflicted many vicious head wounds in retaliation for a defeat suffered the day before in a picket at Emley Moor, where 1,500 pickets had built barricades and forced the police to retreat several times.

Another scene of major battles has been Brodsworth colliery in Yorkshire. On 12 October 3,500 riot police were present and drove armoured vans at high speed towards picket lines, along with cavalry charges. Trevor Womersley was chased on horseback, and batoned to the ground. Police who carried on clubbing him were only driven off by miners

'We ought to pledge ourselves again to the complete emancipation of labour. Because the emancipation of labour, the fight for socialism, is intertwined indissolubly with the fight for the national liberation of Ireland. In the words of James Connolly, and these should be remembered by every trade unionist and Labour movement activist in this country, he said: "The cause of labour is the cause of Ireland, and the cause of Ireland is the cause of labour, they cannot be dissevered".'
MALCOLM PITT, PRESIDENT KENT NUM AT THE IRISH SOLIDARITY MOVEMENT WEEKEND 13/14 OCTOBER 1984

throwing stones at them. On 19 October pickets stoned riot police and horses and escaped without arrests by deploying hit and run tactics. On 16 October at Rossington, a police horse-box and following transit deliberately ran on to the pavement and hit a young picket from Frickley colliery, Darren Price, causing him bad head wounds. Pickets were so incensed at this wanton brutality that they smashed up the police station and overturned a car. You don't have to be picketing to be arrested either. For a young miner's official, being from Grimethorpe was enough. Barry Makinson was walking home with his girlfriend when a group of twenty riot police set upon him and beat him to the ground. They also knocked his girlfriend to the ground. They handcuffed Barry on the floor of the police van, then jumped and stamped on him and pulled his head up up by the hair. He was later charged with criminal damage and breach of the peace. This is only one incident among the many police atrocities in Grimethorpe.

> 'Many of the Labour politicians have dangled about in the middle, "there's violence on the one side and violence on the other". Well I say that our union is unambiguous when it says that we are proud of our young miners...'

> 'But also our women, I take the chance on this platform to pay tribute to the women of the British coalfields. Because as in Ireland, as so long ago in the Commune of Paris, in Red Petrograd, in the sierras of Cuba, in every single gigantic social upheaval then the women have refused to accept a submissive role in society.'

> **MALCOLM PITT**

By the end of October police chiefs had made more than one million deployments of police during the strike. At any one time up to 8,000 police have been used. 7,428 arrests have been made and 8,020 charges have been brought against the miners. Of the 2,524 cases dealt with so far there have been 2,034 convictions. Forty-three miners have been imprisoned, with six miners sent to detention centres, nine detained in police custody, two in youth custody and twenty-five given suspended sentences. 1,051 miners have been given punitive fines of more than £50.

New all-embracing charges have been dug up by police like 'besetting' – used in the 1926 General Strike. All that has to be proved is that the accused was part of a picket line near the place of work of a working miner with the intention of compelling him not to go to work. Miners and their supporters collecting money and food for the strikers and their families are being increasingly arrested and harassed by police in yet another attempt to break solidarity with the strike.

While several thousand miners have been injured, many seriously, police can only claim 954 police slightly injured (this includes the smallest scratch) and 68 seriously injured.

CLASS WAR—COURTS AND PRISONS

'And we tell the judges that we, the miners, will discipline the traitors in our class. The courts expose every day that the ruling class and their judges will never give justice to our class... They will try to jail our members and our leaders, they will seize our funds, but they will never destroy the determination of the British miners...' (Jack Collins, Kent NUM Secretary, 14 October)

The High Courts continue to be used as an open instrument of ruling class justice against the miners. While Attorney General Sir Michael Havers is allowed to break sub judice rules on radio with impunity by talking about the NUM's alleged contempt of court, the appeal of nine Yorkshire miners against blanket bail conditions in Notts, was ruled out by a High Court judge. 94.5% of those 1,745 charged in Notts are on conditional bail.

High Court fines NUM and orders seizure of funds

On 10 October, the High Court fined the NUM £200,000 and Scargill £1,000 for contempt of court. An 'anonymous donor' paid off Scargill's fine but the NUM refused to pay the £200,000. On 25 October, a High Court judge ordered the NUM's funds to be sequestrated. Price Waterhouse, the firm of accountants acting for the court, traced £2.8 million of the funds to Ireland where an Irish High Court judge, sitting in his own home, ordered the Bank of Ireland account with the funds to be frozen. In this way, the relationship between the English and Irish ruling class is made abundantly clear. The NUM is due to challenge this ruling at a full hearing. This money together with at least £4 million in the USA was moved by the NUM, as early as March, as a precaution against sequestration. This and other measures taken by the NUM meant that by 11 November, Price Waterhouse had only managed to get their hands on £8,174.

North Derbyshire scab miners are now seeking to stop their area spending any money on the strike, and the National Working Miners Committee is considering sueing individual NUM EC members for the £200,000. In addition South Wales scabs, headed by Tony Holman, are seeking an injunction to get the South Wales strike declared unofficial. No case of simple miners' grievances here, but a highly coordinated campaign to destroy the NUM, funded by the NCB and private business interests.

A FIGHT TO THE FINISH

Every time the NCB breaks off negotiations with the NUM the efforts to create a 'back-to-work' movement are intensified. With Thatcher's declaration that there is now no possibility of a negotiated settlement, the hopes of the ruling class must rest totally on persuading more and more miners to become scabs and break the strike. To the massive and very costly police protection of scabs and the vast propaganda operation conducted by the ruling class press and media has now been added a Christmas bribe of a pay packet of £1,400 for every miner that sells out his fellow workers and returns to work before 19 November. In the first week of this campaign, even according to the NCB's own dubious figures, 1.2% (2,200) of the total workforce has gone back – hardly the kind of surge predicted by the NCB and government ministers. The NUM anyway strongly challenges the validity of the NCB figures.

68

The miners' determination to halt the 'back-to-work' movement reached new heights at Cortonwood on 9 November. The strike began at Cortonwood and it is fitting that eight months later burning barricades, bricks, stones and catapulted ball-bearings were the weapons of resistance used by the miners against police thugs clad in riot gear; against cavalry charges and attacks from range rovers driven at speed into pickets. A police range rover was overturned and set alight, as were two cabins. The police were held at bay and at times driven back over several hours of confrontation. All this so that one scab could go into work.

Police Terror in Grimethorpe

The level of police brutality and police occupation of entire communities during the miners' strike has led increasingly to comparisons being drawn with life in occupied Ireland. In October in the Yorkshire village of Grimethorpe the comparison was forcibly raised when police brutality led the community to fight back using methods long familiar in Ireland.

On Sunday 14 October the police arrested nineteen men and three youths who were bagging coal on a local tip. Although in previous disputes miners have been allowed to collect coal the NCB has changed this policy during the current strike. They called the police who arrived in three armoured riot vans. Numerous riot police in unnumbered boiler suits chased the miners swinging their trucheons. One 14-year-old was handcuffed to a police bike. Such was the ferocity of the police attack that local women on the nearby estate built barricades to try and stop the police vans.

Early the following morning miners fought with police in the pit yard and later, when the NCB brought in loaders to remove the coal that they themselves had dumped there, angry pickets set fire to one of the giant £40,000 machines and destroyed it. As riot vans moved into the area again, a large crowd assembled and moved off to the local police station where they smashed every window and overturned a police car. Two police officers—one a woman—were forced to flee and police reinforcements were rushed in. Confrontations then carried on that evening and the next. The Chief Constable of South Yorkshire raised the comparison with Ireland again when he asserted 'There are no no-go areas in South Yorkshire'.

As in the Six Counties of Ireland, there was no shortage of people stepping in to try and damp down the fire lit by police brutality. A hasty meeting was called between the Police Committee, the police and the local community. So frightened by the community's response were the police that the Deputy Chief Constable apologised 'unreservedly' for police misbehaviour. When George Moore, a member of the Labour controlled police authority told miners to stay away from coal tips as they were NCB property, everybody in the hall just laughed. During the discussion a miner pointed out that nobody condemned David for throwing stones at Goliath. George Moore replied that no one achieved anything by such means. The miner replied 'David did' and got loud applause.

The sham of the police apology at the meeting was shown when that very day, in Rossington, just a few miles away, a young miner was badly injured when a police horsebox was deliberately driven into him.

OLIVIA ADAMSON

The mass rallies held so far have been a demonstration that the fight-back will continue. Scargill made it clear that the strike-breakers will always be regarded as scabs by their colleagues and by their communities. Every time Kinnock's name is mentioned at the rallies the miners and their families react angrily. At the Edinburgh rally, miners in the hall shouted 'where's Kinnock' at the Labour MPs. Donald Dewar of the Labour Shadow cabinet could hardly get started above the hisses and boos from miners angry at Labour's scabbing on their strike.

The political lessons are rapidly being learned. Just as the striking miners have had to make a decisive break with the scabs in the NUM, so it is necessary to make a similar decisive break with the scabs in the Labour Party and trade union movement. If such a decisive break is made then a victory for the miners will lead to the creation of a new fighting labour movement with both sets of scabs firmly placed where they both belong: outside its ranks.

9-12 November 1984

Photo: Police block the way to Orgreave coke works John Sturrock/ Network

GO OUT TO THE PEOPLE!

8

Every stage of the miners' strike exposed not only the 'false friends' of the striking miners and their communities but also their true allies. If the temporary stalemate, which existed between the opposing forces, was to be decisively broken in favour of the striking miners, those real allies had to now take their place alongside the mining communities as part of a fighting force to defeat the NCB, the Thatcher government and those 'false' friends' of the miners who lead the Labour and trade union movement.

The real allies are to be found amongst those who are already facing the Thatcher government's attacks on jobs, living standards, hospitals and basic democratic rights. They are the most oppressed sections of the working class – the unemployed, black people, Irish people, low paid workers, working class women and also those who have, in the course of defending their democratic rights, faced state repression – the Greenham women, students like those fighting fascism at North London Poly, and the many people collecting on the streets for the miners. In other words the support of hundreds of thousands of ordinary people already sympathetic to the striking miners must now be organised into a political force that can decisively break the impasse and take forward not only the miners' strike but the entire working class. The striking miners must go out to the people!

During November the initiative had temporarily passed to the government as the NCB/media sponsored 'back-to-work' movement became a challenge to the unbroken solidarity of the vast majority of the mining communities. By the beginning of December the 'back-to-work' movement had been successfully halted by a combination of militant picketing and determined resistance to Thatcher's national riot police.

The NCB and the government were forced to turn once again to their corrupt courts and ruling class judges in an attempt to destroy the ability of the NUM and its leaders to run the strike. That the judges could blatantly rule in the government's favour and hand over the NUM's funds to government agents is wholly due to the treacherous character of the leaders of the Labour Party and the trade union movement. These opportunists and traitors are the immovable barrier to real solidarity action among those who support the miners within the official Labour and trade union movement. The 3 December NUM delegate conference decisively voted to defy the reactionary courts and

71

called on the TUC for support and to organise industrial action. The TUC refused. It is now clear that if the impasse is to be broken the decisive push will have to come from outside this movement. This is why the miners should now turn to their supporters amongst the ordinary people and organise with them the only political force capable of combating the reactionary alliance of the NCB, the Thatcher government and its agents in the working class movement.

GOVERNMENT'S OFFENSIVE SET BACK
Back-to-work movement fails

The government put great store on the success of the back-to-work movement. They had hopes of the strike being broken by Christmas with half the workforce back at work. This hope did not materialise in spite of the riot police, the hourly media propaganda bulletins and the NCB bribes – the last being a £175 'bonus' – on account from last year's unsettled pay rise. To try and discourage strikers, the government added £1 to the imaginary £15 'strike pay' already deducted from strikers' families' DHSS benefits.

Even at its peak the NCB could only claim that 5,952 miners went back to work in one week – a thousand short of the 7,000 they had hoped for. The decline in the 'back-to-work' movement is shown even in the following NCB concocted figures:

week ending	10 November 1984	2,200
'' ''	17 November 1984	5,019
'' ''	24 November 1984	5,952
'' ''	1 December 1984	2,158
'' ''	8 December 1984	667
'' ''	15 December 1984	477

Needless to say, by 8 December the media propaganda on the 'back-to-work' movement abruptly ceased. Figures at the end of November from an NCB internal report even show that 100 new strikers were now joining the strike each week.

NCB fiddles back-to-work figures

An article in *The Observer* (25 November) showed how NCB figures were deliberately fiddled. For example the NCB figure of 66,409 NUM members working includes 9,100 who are not at work due to illness – that is not at work or on strike. Often NCB area figures include Colliery Overmen and Staff Association COSA (clerical), BACM (managers) and NACODS (pit deputies) members. On 8 December *The Guardian* reported 'despite the fact that 16,383 miners have returned to work since the end of October there has been no big increase in the amount of deep mined coal being produced'. So much for the 'back-to-work' movement.

SCABS AND COURTS COMBINE

The legal system has, with the aid of scab miners, been used as a blatant political weapon against the NUM. It is significant that it is not the Tories' employment legislation which has been used in the attacks on the miners' union, but the 'normal' civil law of Britain, manipulated by a treacherously corrupt and vicious ruling class judiciary.

The NUM now faces 20 or more legal actions in the courts. Scab miners, funded from a whole number of right wing sources, including private businessmen, Aims of Industry, Moral Rearmament, are assisted by a range of similarly minded solicitors and journalists. Also deeply involved in advising the scab miners' committees are two of Thatcher's aides – Tim Bell of Saatchi and Saatchi (who also advises MacGregor) and David Hart. Hart, whose merchant banker father worked at one time with MacGregor, was described by a miner who left a scab miners' committee in disgust:

> 'He was handing over sums of up to £300 in cash as floats. In my opinion, Hart was not acting as an adviser, he was running the show'.

The appointment of the accountants Price Waterhouse to sequestrate the NUM funds took place during October, due to so-called 'contempt of court' by NUM leaders after failure to pay the £200,000 fine imposed in October. The sequestrators reported to the High Court on 28 November that £2.78m of NUM funds had been located in Dublin, £4.63m in Luxembourg and £503,000 in Zurich. Three days later the High Court took the unprecedented step of declaring Arthur Scargill, Peter Heathfield and Mick McGahey 'unfit persons' to be trustees of NUM funds and removed them, appointing a receiver in their place. The receiver appointed was Herbert Brewer, a Derbyshire solicitor, chairman of a local Tory Party, a director of several companies and a freemason. The High Court refused the NUM's appeal against this gross anti-working class measure the following day. In response the NUM called an emergency delegate conference on 3 December where it was decided to

John Sturrock/Network

continue to defy the courts and not to bring money back to Britain to pay the fines. This conference also called for TUC support in what Scargill called 'an attempt to hijack the union'. Following the ludicrous Brewer's failure to return any NUM funds to Britain, a new receiver has been appointed – Michael Arnold of Arthur Young Mc-Lelland Moores. The government itself has now decided to underwrite the expenses of the receiver to avoid any further embarrassment. Such open interference in legal matters reveals once again that the ruling class abandons any pretence of the 'neutrality of the law' when it ceases to be useful for its purposes.

An attempt being made in the High Court to appoint a receiver for the NUM Yorkshire funds – said to be even greater than the national fund – was adjourned on 13 December until March. The insidious action by two North Derbyshire scabs to seek a High Court order to force 3 officials in their local area NUM to pay back £1.7 million used for the strike, failed on 14 December. Even here the judge accepted the scabs' arguments that the strike was unlawful and that the local officials were personally liable to repay £1.7m, but he would not grant such an order.

In addition, during November, as well as making illegal a 50p levy imposed by the National Union of Seamen on its members, the High Court stopped students from North London Poly Students Union making a donation to the miners. The High Court also turned down an appeal by four striking Yorkshire miners that police road blocks into

Barrister wins right to collect

Notts were illegal. One significant victory took place in a test case at a Magistrates court in London where Barrister James Wood, himself accused of making an illegal collection for the miners in Bloomsbury, London, was found not guilty of the charge.

STATE TERROR CONTINUES

The government/NCB have continued to use police terror to get scabs into work. It is remarkable that police, who say they do not have the forces to protect Asian families from racist attacks, can provide whole units to protect a single scab and his family. Renewed battles between riot police and pickets, begun at Cortonwood on 9 November, have continued almost daily in Yorkshire and South Wales on an unprece-dented scale. Barricades have been lit, trenches dug, bricks and petrol bombs have been thrown – in order to prevent the 'back-to-work' movement from breaking the strike. This has to a great extent been successful. Police have launched vicious attacks on entire communi-ties just as in the Six Counties of Ireland. In Rossington (12 Novem-ber) and Thurnscoe (20 November) in Yorkshire, police ran amok and forced their way into Miners Welfare Clubs, viciously beating miners to the ground and, in the latter case, dragging out a 13 year old boy.

In contrast to the almost total silence in the media on the activities of the police and the occupation of the pit villages has been the hysteria over strikers' anger against scabs who have betrayed their com-munities and their class. Once again, on 26 November, Thatcher and Brittan took up the campaign to equate miners – their so-called

74

'enemy within' – with the **IRA**. This refrain, together with that equating Scargill with Oswald Mosley – 'left fascism' – are the government's crude attempts to isolate miners from their supporters among people in all areas of the country.

LABOUR LEADERS HOLD BACK STRIKE

TUC and Labour Party leaders have not only stood silent while mining communities – women, children and men – have been beaten up in their communities and on the picket lines – they have *actively* sought to bring about the defeat of the miners. Small wonder that it is reported that NUM branches and many individual miners are leaving

Out picketing

Pit Lane already had two trenches which the police had filled in the previous night. But this night the trench could not be filled in in a hurry—it was about 2 foot deep and about 3 foot wide. A group of youths began to gather together at the far pit gate to build a barricade as a final line of defence to stop the one scab that goes into Kinsley Drift. The youths donned balaclavas and masks as they warmed themselves around the picket fire. The work began after all hellos had been said and stories told about the previous night's incidents with the police. Tactics were also talked.

Girders were found to put at the bottom of the barricade and pallets were put on top. The girders had got really hot the previous night and couldn't be lifted out of the way. The barricade was built about 15 yards away from the pit gates. A posse went off around the pit top to look for some diesel. We came across security men. We pulled up our masks and made sure our faces could not be seen. But they moved off in the other direction when they saw us. Eventually the barricade was up. Someone had put some canisters in the barricade so there were a few unexpected explosions.

We could see the lights of the convoys of police vans on the horizon. Eleven vans in one convoy to bring the scabs in. We knew the police would be here soon. A fence was ripped down to try and get a Portakabin out to put right in between the gateposts. Twelve of us heaved and pulled until it was felled. Two pickets kept a look out at a side road which led to some allotments. Dogs were barking up there so trouble could be coming. Three figures appeared in the gateway out of the darkness—one lookout said that it was the lads so it was alright. But it wasn't the lads and it wasn't alright . . . Rows of shining riot helmets appeared, and dogs. Their leader shouted 'Get the bastards!' They hesitated but we didn't and ran back to the picket hut. The rest of the pickets near the barricade were cut off as 120-150 riot clad police charged them. They scattered and ran but managed to throw a couple of canisters on to the barricade which exploded once the police thought everything was over! It scared them to put it mildly! The pickets ran for hours, evading the beatings they would receive once captured. Not one was caught.

Finally, at 4.30am, a couple of hours after all the chasing was over, the scab slowly crawled to Kinsley Drift in the back of a police van. He ran up with his head under a blanket. No one sees him except the police. This week Sussex were here—next week the Met is coming up!

AN FRFI SUPPORTER

the Labour Party in disgust. Kinnock, who referred with contempt to the strike as a 'potential Gallipoli', while doing his best to sabotage it, had the nerve while he was in Moscow, to tell Soviet miners that the reports of British miners' families starving were exaggerated. At a 6,000 strong rally in South Wales in November which Kinnock was 'too busy' to attend, a banner appeared asking 'Where's Ramsey MacKinnock?' At the same rally, a noose was lowered down in front of Norman Willis, TUC General Secretary, who had come to the rally to condemn 'the brick, the bolt and the petrol bomb'. Willis's speech

Noose lowered in front of Willis

was abruptly ended as the noose was lowered, drowned out by a united and continuous chanting of 'Here we go, here we go, here we go . . .'. The next day Kinnock, Hattersley and a battery of trade union leaders rushed to sympathise with Willis and to attack those men and women who dared to criticise such as they. The noose symbolised a rejection of all that these foul opportunists stand for – their refusal to fight, their subservience to the ruling class and its courts and police. The noose also signified that they cannot be reformed – they must and will be swept to one side.

After the NUM's decision to defy the courts at its special delegate

TUC says it will not take illegal action

conference on 3 December, the TUC met miners' leaders. The TUC announced it could give no help to the miners other than 'encouraging' members to take industrial action in support of the miners, and further they could not undertake *any* action which would bring them into contempt of the law, such as openly offering premises or wages to NUM workers. On the same day Kinnock too said that the Labour Party could not contemplate breaking the law.

Despite Arthur Scargill's appeals over the heads of union leaders to their members, the organised labour movement has not responded and remains deeply divided over support for the miners.

Some manual workers at power stations at Didcot, West Thurrock and in Yorkshire, are refusing to handle scab coal, and railway workers at one main depot at Coalville in Leicestershire are refusing to move coal. Apart from this, solidarity actions still remain at an abysmally low level. In contrast, masked squads of French CGT miners overturned railway wagons carrying coal at Marseilles and Calais in an act of real solidarity with their British comrades.

CLASS WAR PRISONERS

'There are a lot of miners who have been picked up and locked up in prison today and if I have one criticism of the NUM . . . it's this: they have not yet thought out clearly their position in relation to their imprisoned comrades and that is a grave weakness . . . will they be forgotten about or is it just a memory, a demonstration outside the prisons now and again? How are their comrades to behave when they are locked in prison . . . If they are political prisoners obviously they must then fight for political status within the prison, that is something that the miners, as far as I know, haven't yet thought about . . . ' (John McCluskey, Irish POW, at Irish Solidarity Movement conference 14 October 1985)

By early December 8,731 miners had been arrested (this does not include supporters), 87 miners had been gaoled and 17 sent to detention centres. In addition large numbers of miners are being held on remand – over 100 in Armley prison Leeds. The first woman, Brenda Greenwood, has been gaoled for defying bail conditions. Hundreds more miners face almost certain prison sentences, some of them very lengthy ones. These include miners arrested for attacks on scabs and also the two miners charged with the murder of the scab taxi driver in South Wales. In the face of the wholesale 'criminalisation' of the mining communities in struggle, an urgent task confronts these communities and their supporters: the building of political and material support for the prisoners and their families.

The miners are the largest group of workers so far in Britain to go to gaol as class war prisoners. As the class struggle intensifies thousands more are bound to follow. The British prison system is barbaric and uncivilised and refuses to acknowledge the existence of political and class war prisoners. 12 Irish political prisoners have died on hunger strike in their rightful struggle for political status – 2 of them in English gaols. Des Warren, the Shrewsbury building worker, gaoled in 1973 under the Conspiracy and Protection of Property Act 1875, went on hunger strike in early 1974 for 22 days in his fight for political status. This was refused by a Labour government.

The miners in prison must organise to defend themselves and the rights of class war prisoners. They will find experienced allies in the Irish and black prisoners who have carried out a consistent struggle over many years in defence of their own interests and those of all prisoners. The miners will find many of the ordinary prisoners they meet sympathetic to their struggle. For these prisoners suffer equally under the yoke of the capitalist system, its laws, courts and barbaric prison regime.

Miners' rally – Edinburgh

The leadership of the NUM launched a nation-wide tour of key areas on 6 November in Edinburgh. Against the backdrop of stepped-up hostility from the Labour and TUC leadership, the first in the series of rallies was marked by jeers from the 2000+ miners present. These were hurled when NUM leader and Communist Party head, Mick McGahey began reading out Labour apologies for non-attendance. The shout 'Kinnock's a Tory' made McGahey move quickly to say that Tories didn't send apologies to NUM rallies. This was one of the first of many outbursts from the audience which McGahey sought to smooth away. After Labour MP Gavin Strang had spoken, miners in the hall challenged 'Where's Kinnock?' Donald Dewar of the Labour Party Shadow Cabinet could hardly get started above the hisses and boos vented by miners angry at Labour's scabbing on their strike. Eurocommunist McGahey quietened the hall down again so that Dewar could tell miners that 'we all condemn violence'. Before this we were treated to the sickening charity of John Henry (Assistant General Secretary of the Scottish TUC, to give him his full title). He told the miners that whilst they (the STUC) 'couldn't ensure turkey and all the trimmings for Christmas' they'd make sure that 'everyone of yous will sit down to a chicken or something else.' I reckon that the food off their (the STUC) Christmas tables would go a long way to meeting more than just the Christmas needs of many miners' families. In the circumstances of Kinnock's point-blank scabbing on attendance at the rallies (although he can make time to fly to India in Mrs Thatcher's jet) Arthur Scargill's remark that his engagement diary was not block-booked, ie unlike Kinnock's, was very mild. Yet this received resounding applause.
November 1984

The class struggle on the outside must not end at the prison gate. If it is not carried on inside the prison by those who have shown themselves to be the most resolute fighters for their class, then it can lead to demoralisation on the outside. For those facing the daily threat of imprisonment for fighting the class struggle must be confident in the knowledge that should they be sent to prison they will join their comrades and many others to continue the class struggle on the inside. As the experience of every revolutionary struggle has shown, the prisons will become training schools for the future revolutionary movement.

A political movement can be assessed by the way it looks after and organises support for its prisoners. Urgent work must be carried out in setting up prisoners support groups throughout the country. Every miner in prison must know that there are those on the outside who organise political and material support and who are ready to publicly respond to any attack or any denial of democratic rights the prison system may impose on miners. Miners' relatives and friends have to play a central role in building these support groups. Revolutionaries have a vitally important task in helping to bring this about. Imprisoned miners and these groups will have to conduct a political fight for the recognition of class war prisoners in the British prison system and for the freeing of all political prisoners. The lessons learnt today will serve the working class movement well in the future.

GO OUT TO THE PEOPLE!

The organised working class movement has failed to give the kind of active solidarity that could have already led to a victory for the miners. The leaders of the Labour and trade union movement feel themselves under no significant pressure to organise any further support. On the contrary they are doing their utmost to force the miners to accept an unprincipled compromise with the NCB, hence the eagerness of the TUC, on Friday 14 December, to grovel before Peter Walker, the Energy Secretary, and plead with him to restart negotiations.

While revolutionaries must continue to fight for and build active solidarity with the miners within the organised trade union movement, a new emphasis must now be given to going out to build new fighting alliances outside that movement.

Soon after the beginning of the strike Arthur Scargill, on 28 March 1984, said of the Tory government:

'They know they are in largely uncharted land because this dispute is mainly about jobs, and waiting in the wings are four million unemployed whose numbers could swell the picket lines at any time.'

Unfortunately, the work necessary to bring this about has never been done. For the organised trade union movement has systematically isolated and ignored the growing ranks of the unemployed. Likewise, miners have spoken of significant support amongst black people for the strike. Yet little has been done to draw on these powerful potential allies in their struggle. Besides this, thousands of low paid workers and women workers, ignored and appallingly treated by the organised labour movement over the years, are willing to make their contribution to the fight.

Support groups throughout the country have played a central role in providing material assistance for the miners' strike. While this is vital, the support groups must begin to play a more substantial political role in support of the strike and for the defeat of the Thatcher government. The miners and their supporters must build such groups with the aim of drawing in all these new forces into their struggle in every town, city and mining community in the country.

Revolutionaries have to help turn these support groups into fightng organisations that can begin to exert a new pressure on the labour movement to back the strike and to force the Thatcher government into a retreat. These support groups must organise more public meetings and local demonstrations to draw in new forces in support of the miners and counter with leaflets and regular bulletins the vile propaganda put out by the government controlled media. In the major urban centres pickets could be organised on police stations – this could be particularly effective if coordinated with NUM mass pickets. This would stretch the resources of the police and take some of the pressure off the picket lines. Local demonstrations can have the same effect. This could be of real significance in London whose hated Metropolitan Police have played a savage role in brutalising miners and their supporters. Support groups should continue to visit mining communities and join the picket lines if requested. This has now to be done in a more systematic way.

These support groups could organise material support for and defence of prisoners and regular pickets of prisons where there are miners inside. They could put pressure on local Labour councils, Labour councillors and Labour MPs to be more active in support of the miners strike – picketing Labour council meetings, MPs' and councillors' surgeries if necessary. Such developments would not only have a significant impact on the strike but would play a constructive role in starting the process of rebuilding the working class movement in Britain.

14-15 December 1984

The Left and the miners' strike

The repeated calls for a General Strike by Trotskyists and sections of the Labour Party left are not only unrealistic in the face of the TUC and Labour Party's cowardly refusal to break the law, they are dangerous, and could lead to demoralisation and inactivity. A failed General Strike, in the unlikely event of one being called, would bring certain victory for the government and the NCB as every major union would split in two. And this would be used as yet a further excuse for the Labour leaders to isolate Arthur Scargill and the striking miners.

The headlines in most of the Trotskyist papers are calls to the dead to breathe: 'TUC get off your knees' (Socialist Worker 7 December), 'TUC must back the miners—Call a 24 hour General Strike!' (Socialist Action 7 December), 'Organise a General Strike to back the miners' (Newsline, every day), 'General Strike needed to defend union rights' (Militant 7 December). While the Trotskyist left resorts to wishful thinking the Morning Star simply lies. 'TUC pledges "we will keep NUM going"' was the headline on the very day after the TUC's decision that 'blatantly' offering the NUM new premises, running costs and payment of wages of NUM staff 'could not be contemplated' (Morning Star, 7 December).

All these organisations of the left refuse to acknowledge a fundamental split in the working class movement. First they sow illusions in the ability of the trade union leadership to deliver the goods amongst those who want the miners to win. When their wishful thinking fails to materialise no doubt we will be subjected to self-righteous sermons about the 'betrayers' of the strike. The high priests of Trotskyism—the Revolutionary Communist Party (RCP)—have already renounced any contact with material reality. Not only have they scabbed throughout the strike by calling for a national ballot, they now have a long list of betrayers of the 'miners' battle for jobs'. Chief among them is Arthur Scargill.

The call now for a General Strike is in fact an evasion of the real responsibilities and tasks facing revolutionaries in relation to the strike. This demands facing up to reality and building support for the miners amongst sections of the working class which have everything to gain from the miners victory. And, as has already been demonstrated throughout the nine months of the miners' strike, that support cannot be limited to the organised working class. To go forward the strike must go out to the people—to the more oppressed sections of the working class.

15 DECEMBER 1984

BUILDING FOR THE FUTURE

9

The class struggle will not tolerate a lengthy stalemate between opposing forces. By the third week in January, December's temporary impasse in the miners' strike was broken. The initiative once again passed back to Thatcher and the NCB. Despite the unprecedented and heroic eleven-month struggle of the striking miners, their families and communities, the growing split in the NUM, the absence of active solidarity from key sections of the trade union movement and the purposeful scabbing by leaders of the Labour Party and TUC left the mining communities with their backs against the wall.

But the fight will go on. A negotiated settlement will not and cannot be the end of the miners' strike. For whatever the conditions the NUM finally accept for a return to work, the political gains achieved in the hard-fought struggle will remain.

The mining communities and hundreds of thousands of their supporters, have come to understand the vicious class character of the British imperialist state as they have experienced its police, courts and prisons. Many now recognise the need for disciplined organisation to defend themselves against it. Forced themselves to fight with the brick, the barricade and the petrol bomb against Thatcher's national riot police, they have come for the first time to see allies in those fighting for freedom in the Six Counties of Ireland and in black people forced to fight against the racist police state in Britain.

Thousands of workers have come to know the character of the leadership of the Labour Party and trade union movement and to realise that a new fighting movement can only be built after a decisive break with these leaders and the section of the working class which follows them. Perhaps the most important political development in the strike has been the critical and often leading role of the women in the mining communities in defending and sustaining the strike through organisation, demonstrations, street activities and defence of their relatives and friends in prison. A lasting advance for the miners and the working class movement can only be won if these gains are consolidated.

THATCHER WANTS NUM SURRENDER

Knowing the danger that a Scargill-led miners' victory would mean for the ruling class, Thatcher has shown that she is prepared to go to any lengths and to bear any costs necessary to beat the miners' strike. In

July last year her Chancellor of the Exchequer, Nigel Lawson, described the already large extra costs due to the strike as 'a worthwhile investment for the good of the nation' – by which he meant the gang of British
and international profiteers whose interests Thatcher represents.

The costs are mounting rapidly. Already it seems likely that
government spending for 1984/5 will overshoot expenditure plans by
some £3.3bn – jeopardising the tax handouts that the Tory government had earmarked for its wealthy friends. At least £1.5bn of this
extra expenditure was attributable to the miners' strike up till Christmas. Another £500m will be added if the strike continues into March.
Andrew Glyn, an Oxford economist, has estimated that the *total* cost

**Strike costs
£5 billion**

of the miners' strike so far is a massive £5bn, when all hidden costs including loss of output, taxation and increased social security payments
are taken into account.

Much of the extra cost has been in the production of electricity. In
her determination to avoid power cuts Thatcher has sanctioned unlimited spending. Spending on oil soars every day as the dollar strengthens
and the pound weakens. In December 1984 the CEGB was burning
eight times as much oil as in a normal December at a minimum cost of
some £40m a week. Gas turbines, which are even more expensive to use
than oil in the production of electricity, are normally used for only a
few days a year to meet peak demand. It is now estimated that they are
being used at least one day out of two. Further costs result from the
extensive use of scab lorries to move coal and oil to power stations. In
the Notts coalfield, due to the refusal of some groups of railway
workers to move coal, an estimated 12,000 lorryloads a day are being
used to supply coal to the vital Trent Valley power stations.

All this shows that Thatcher is determined to force a crushing
defeat on the miners and Arthur Scargill. Nothing less than total
surrender will satisfy her.

At every stage, when negotiations have looked like ending in a
compromise agreement acceptable to the NUM, Thatcher has stepped
in to prevent such an outcome. Even now, when new negotiations had
been informally agreed to by NUM General Secretary Peter Heathfield and Ned Smith of the NCB, Thatcher has publicly insisted that no
negotiations take place before an NUM written surrender on the issue
of uneconomic pits. In an interview on ITV on 24 January she said,
'The NCB has to manage . . . the NCB has to close uneconomic pits. It
always has. It has decisions to take. That has to be clear from the out-
set'. She dismisses any talk of independent arbitration boards on pit
closures. Such bodies can only be 'consultative' she said – that is, we'll
ignore them if they don't satisfy our requirements.

Sections of the ruling class, worried about the effects of the miners'
strike on the economy and international confidence in the pound – its
value has fallen by some 20% during the course of the strike – are

**Thatcher
prevents
settlement**

arguing for compromise. Thatcher is determined to push aside this
pressure and go out for total victory. Sections of the NCB management, anxious about the long-term effects of the strike on the industry, are also trying to find a negotiating position which stops short
of demanding total defeat for the striking miners. They are only

too aware that, on their own estimate, a hard core of at least 40% of the NUM (75,000) are prepared to stay out indefinitely, leaving the NCB with an impossible operational problem. MacGregor, however, was not hired at a cost of millions to provide friendly agreements. He was brought in by Thatcher to break the union in order to slash the size of the industry, leaving only highly profitable pits. Thatcher confirmed this on 25 January when she refused to deny that the vast majority of pits in the older coalfields, like those of Kent, South Wales and Scotland, would almost certainly be closed.

In spite of Thatcher's forceful intervention, the NUM Executive's public declaration on 24 January that they were prepared to restart negotiations with no preconditions has pressurised the NCB into agreeing to have talks about a possible agenda for future negotiations. These will start on Tuesday 29 January.

There can be no doubt that if the miners are forced back on terms

Photo: Women organise to save jobs and communities
John Sturrock/Network

83

acceptable to Thatcher, tens of thousands of jobs will be lost, and scores of pits closed. Arthur Scargill's predictions at the beginning of the strike, about MacGregor's plans for the coal industry, were no exaggeration. Thatcher cannot be allowed to win. The strike cannot be ended on her terms. It is imperative that this message is put over to the trade union movement and to the masses of ordinary people who support the miners in a major effort to once again raise the tempo of resistance.

THREAT TO LABOUR'S CHANCES?

Thatcher is fighting a class war. She is determined to defend the interests of her class. Labour Party leader, Kinnock, and TUC General Secretary, Willis, know nothing of class war and seek only class collaboration, that is, peace at any price. Of primary concern to them, far more important than the miners' strike, is the Labour Party's popularity and its prospects at the next General Election – in other words the career prospects and status of themselves and their friends. The determined and militant fightback of the striking miners and their communities is nothing but an embarrassment to these leaders. To have taken the side of the striking miners, at any time, on the fundamental issues raised in the course of the strike – workers' democracy *v* ruling class democracy, workers' violence *v* police violence, illegality *v* legality – would, they believe, have° undermined Labour's respectability in the capitalist media's popularity polls.

The miners' strike has become such a threat to Kinnock and those he represents that when a group of left Labour MPs staged a demonstration in the House of Commons calling on the government for a debate on the strike (something which Kinnock too had opposed as 'not helpful' at the present time – that is, not 'helpful' to Kinnock) the sitting was suspended for 20 minutes. Kinnock later rounded on these MPs, the handful that have supported the miners, with vicious fury, accusing them of 'utter indiscipline' and 'self indulgence'. This action by Kinnock, supported by most Labour MPs, shows without a doubt that the Labour Party will not defend the interests of ordinary people in struggle even within the narrow confines of the parliamentary debating chamber. Labour MPs, if they are worth anything, should have been disrupting parliament, day after day, to put the miners' case.

Kinnock attacks 'Labour lefts'

The continuation of the strike daily opens up the split in the working class movement and destroys bit by bit the ability of leaders like Kinnock and Willis to pose as representatives of the whole working class. In a TUC debate on 17 December a terrifying spectre was raised: according to the TUC a failure to achieve a clear settlement in the strike could mean that 10-30,000 miners might 'permanently' stay out on strike. TUC leaders thought that this would present 'a dangerous feature which had never been witnessed before'. Dangerous indeed for the position of the likes of Kinnock and Willis that a significant section of the organised working class might break free of their stranglehold. The leaders of the Labour and trade union movement have shown throughout the strike that they have everything to lose from a Scargill-led victory.

84

The split in the working class over the miners' strike is not just between the reactionary leaders like Kinnock, Willis, Basnett and Duffy, and the rank and file workers, but is a split that has gone deep down into the movement as workers have taken sides according to where their immediate interests lie. For every railway worker who has refused to move coal there have been others who have moved it, and hundreds of scab TGWU lorry drivers, earning in many cases over £1,000 a week, have profited from the strike. On the other hand railway workers at the key Coalville depot in Leicestershire who have blocked the movement of coal all the way through the strike fought for weeks to get mass support for their stand from their unions. Two were sacked and others disciplined for alleged theft; a signalman was sent home by management because he was said to be 'mentally unstable'. His absence was used to deploy a scabbing member from the newly formed 'Federation of Professional Railway Staff' to allow coal trains through for the first time in 10 months during December. A successful one day rail strike was called in support of the Coalville workers on 17 January in the Yorkshire and East Midlands region. And 200 workers at Waterloo station in London walked out against their unions' wishes.

At the power stations, key electricians and power workers have categorically refused to aid the miners, even with action that does not involve strikes. The scabbing of these workers has undermined the action of other groups of power station workers in the TGWU and the AUEW. 200 AUEW workers at Didcot power station have now abandoned their decision not to handle coal supplies.

What Thatcher and Kinnock, MacGregor and Willis have in common is a single-minded determination to isolate and defeat Arthur Scargill and the class politics he has put forward during the miners' strike. They must do this to prevent the split in the working class movement going deep enough to begin the process of creating a new fighting movement. Such a movement would be a pole of attraction for thousands and thousands of workers disgusted with the politics of the Labour Party and TUC and their leaders Kinnock and Willis.

DEFEND THE GAINS OF THE STRIKE

The period after Christmas has seen a massive propaganda effort by the government and the NCB to bring about a mass return to work. Adverts placed in local and Sunday newspapers, personal letters to strikers, added to Thatcher's total refusal to contemplate negotiations (for nearly three months), have been clearly designed to exert maximum pressure on strikers faced with a new year of hardship for themselves and their families. The propaganda campaign has been waged particularly hard in South Wales where only 281 (342 NCB figure) out of 19,600 miners are at work.

NCB figures for the return to work since the New Year show some 9,230 men back at work for the first time:

MS–G

week ending (three days)	4 January	705
'' ''	11 January	2269
'' ''	18 January	2870
'' ''	25 January	3386

Back-to-work movement gains ground

While this is lower than the return to work rate in November and even allowing for the usual exaggeration by the NCB, this return to work still presents a major problem for the NUM. How the NUM responds to this is critical. In November the return to work was halted by mass picketing. So far a similar response has not been organised. This has allowed the less determined and less committed members of the NUM Executive to exert more pressure on Arthur Scargill and his supporters. One result has been the decision that the whole Executive takes part in the next set of negotiations with the NCB – clearly a weakening of the NUM's ability to hold out on the fundamental issues at stake. For some of the NUM Executive have wanted to end the strike at every available opportunity.

Another pressure on the NUM leaders is that the split in the NUM between strikers and scabs could lead to the formation of a breakaway union. The Notts area NUM decided to delete rule 30, which asserts the supremacy of the National Executive and rule book over that of the local area. Similar developments are taking place in the small areas of Leicestershire and South Derbyshire. In Notts the pro-strike General Secretary Henry Richardson was dismissed from his post, and in South Derbyshire striking miners have been expelled from the union. While efforts and concessions are being made to prevent the split, a continuation of the strike could lead to the formation of a

Photo: 'What Thatcher and Kinnock, MacGregor and Willis have in common is a single-minded determination to isolate and defeat Arthur Scargill and the class politics he has put forward during the miners' strike'. John Sturrock/ Network

bosses' union which MacGregor and the NCB have said they are prepared to recognise.

It is crucial at this state, when negotiations are being considered, to step up active support for the strike, both inside and outside the NUM. The new organisations which have been built during the strike – the women's support groups in the mining areas, and the miners' support groups in the towns and cities – can be consolidated in the next few weeks and start the process of winning back the initiative from Thatcher and the NCB. Mass pickets need to be organised again and a campaign to raise funds for this purpose must get under way. For some time now miners in key areas like Yorkshire have been bitterly complaining that funds for picketing, petrol expenses, and vans have been withdrawn by NUM officials. Such officials can be by-passed.

Food and material aid collections must be stepped up on a country-wide basis. Leading figures in the NUM and left Labour MPs who support the miners must go out to the people *outside* the mining areas to help bring this about. Many miners are being forced back to work through hardship, cold and hunger. This could be stopped if the necessary funds were collected. The miners' support groups have a key role in making this possible. Mass rallies, demonstrations and street collections should be organised throughout the country to build support for the miners amongst the mass of ordinary people who want to see Thatcher defeated. Don't allow labour movement officialdom and 'defeatism' to get in the way.

The women's support groups show what can be achieved. They are not waiting for permission from union officials to organise in support of the strike. In the last two weeks a three day march has been organised by a miners' wives support group in North Derbyshire, a mass picket and thousand-strong demonstration by the women at Hatfield Main colliery in Yorkshire. This repeated all over the country over the next few weeks would take the initiative out of the hands of those who do not want to carry on the fight.

The women's support groups in the mining areas and the miners' support groups in the towns and cities are a major gain of the strike. Their continued work will be crucial after the strike ends to prevent victimisation of strikers and to defend imprisoned miners. Increased activity now will mean that solid organisation and experience exists to defend miners and other workers in the future. In Islington a small number of determined local activists (including FRFI comrades) collected nearly £800 on a mobile street collection for Soutn Wales miners, built a demonstration of 1,500 people and have organised a picket on Wandsworth prison where a Kent miner has started a five-year gaol sentence – all in a period of a few weeks. Their success has encouraged many new people to be active in support of the miners.

After the strike ends a political task of enormous importance will face those who have supported the strike: the defence of class war prisoners and the reinstatement of those sacked by the NCB as a result of convictions in the courts. Already 150 miners have been sentenced to gaol – one of them for 5 years and many more will follow. Over 500 miners have been sacked as a result of convictions in the courts. If

150 miners gaoled

these class war fighters are not resolutely defended then this and future struggles will be held back. The Fitzwilliam Prisoners Aid Committee is showing the way. This group of miners, miners' wives and supporters (including FRFI comrades) has begun the work of defending local prisoners. Other groups must follow their lead and use their experience.

Whatever takes place over the next few weeks, whether the strike ends or not, the work must go on so the heroic struggle of the striking miners, their families and communities leads to lasting gains for the whole working class.

25-26 January 1985

Class war prisoners

In the last fierce class struggle here—which was the period of strikes and working class militancy leading up to the 1926 General Strike—hundreds of workers were jailed for long periods of hard labour.

The setting up of the British section of the International Class War Prisoners Aid (ICWPA) in 1925 was a response to the clear need to defend and support the prisoners—in particular leading Communists charged with sedition for calling on the armed forces not to fire on workers in struggle. The ICWPA also took up the defence of South Wales anthracite miners who had had vicious sentences imposed in an attempt to crush their struggle.

The campaign of the British working class to defend its prisoners was made in common cause with the international struggle—particularly the anti-imperialist struggles of the Indian and Irish people against British rule. Rallies up and down the country in February 1925 were addressed by the black Communist MP Shapurji Saklatvala, and by Jim Larkin, leader of the Dublin workers during the 1913 lock-out. Saklatvala was able to present to Parliament a petition of 300,000 signatures, gathered in just over one month, which demanded the instant release of all class war prisoners.

On Release the Prisoners Day, 7 February 1926, 15,000 marched from Clapham over the common to Wandsworth prison where the Communist leaders were held. On 7 March of the same year, a mass solidarity rally packed the Albert Hall.

As miners today go to prison, they will find allies amongst those who have been in the vanguard of the struggle for prisoners' rights—Irish political prisoners, black prisoners and others who have fought against solitary confinement, censorship, druggings and beatings.

The inevitable struggle against criminalisation inside the prisons can only be successful if a campaign in solidarity is built outside. In this, the women who have built the miners wives support groups will undoubtedly play a major role—just as the women of the nationalist working class in Ireland built the Relatives Action Committees to mobilise their people against the criminalisation of the H-Block prisoners.

FRFI has always committed itself to support the struggle for prisoners' rights and against the criminalisation of political prisoners. Our newspaper will be a friend and ally to any miner imprisoned for fighting for his class, and to their families on the outside.

MAGGIE MELLON, PAULINE SELLARS

MINERS FORCED BACK

one year of heroic struggle

Almost one year to the day after MacGregor announced the NCB's pit closure programme, a national delegate conference of the NUM decided on 3 March on an organised return to work for Tuesday 5 March. The Executive was evenly split and made no recommendation. But by 98-91 votes the delegates decided to go back and to seek an amnesty for the more than 700 miners sacked. So ended the most heroic strike the British working class had seen for decades.

By the end of January the initiative had passed to Thatcher and the NCB. However, in spite of the confident forecast by government ministers and media that the strike would end at that time, the predicted 'surge' back to work did not reach anything like the peak levels of November 1984, when nearly 6,000 miners went back in one week.

By mid-February the Thatcher government was coming under pressure due to: the escalating costs of the strike, rising at some £55m-£60m a week; a turnaround in the current account balance of payments from a forecast £2bn surplus to a £200m deficit; and a reduction in the growth rate of the economy by some 2%. Leaked CEGB figures showed the huge cost of avoiding power cuts by burning oil. Last year the Electricity Board made £200m profit – the forecast for this year is a staggering £2,000m loss. In addition the miners' strike has certainly played some part in the falling pound and record interest rates which have wrecked the Tory financial strategy.

Strike costs soar

Opinion polls in mid-February showed a marked fall in the Thatcher government's popularity. With the damaging political defeat for the government after an Old Bailey jury acquitted Clive Ponting in the Ministry of Defence secrets case, and the threat of industrial action by teachers and other workers looming ahead, sections of the ruling class believed it was time for a negotiated settlement of the miners' strike. Thatcher, however, was still determined to inflict a humiliating defeat on Arthur Scargill and the striking miners. And she had one crucial card to play. The TUC leadership was equally determined to see an end to the strike and a return to 'normality'. The doors to MacGregor, Walker and even Thatcher herself were suddenly opened to Willis and the TUC leaders. Their role was to be decisive in finally breaking the back of the strike.

TUC OPPORTUNISTS DO THEIR DIRTY WORK

At the end of January Thatcher and MacGregor demanded that before negotiations could start the NUM had to give a written guarantee that the closure of 'uneconomic' pits should be the central item on the agenda. The NUM refused, and preliminary talks between Peter Heathfield, NUM General Secretary, and the NCB broke down. The NUM pointed out that such a precondition invalidated the NCB/NACODS agreement of October 1984 which introduced a new independent colliery review procedure in the case of a dispute over the closure of pits. NACODS Secretary, Peter McNestry, even went through the motions of threatening to ballot his members for strike action if the NCB refused to withdraw the demand for a written guarantee. On 6 February a joint meeting of the Executive Committees of NACODS and the NUM made a demand for talks without any preconditions. This demand was rejected by the government and the NCB. Once again Thatcher's intervention prevented any negotiations taking place.

TUC and NCB produce 8 point document

It was at this point that Willis stepped in. He had been having secret talks with MacGregor and the NCB, resulting on 15 February in an 8 point document which effectively spelt out the NCB terms for a settlement. Central to it was the acceptance of the right of the NCB to close 'uneconomic' pits. For example, item 2 of the TUC/NCB document states:

'The NUM recognise that it is the duty of the NCB to manage the industry efficiently, and to secure sound developments in accordance with their responsibilities and the NCB recognise that the NUM represents and advances the interests of its members and their employment opportunities. In this regard the NCB is firmly of the view that the interests of the membership of the NUM are best served by the development of an economically sound industry.'

As for the modified independent review procedure the document clearly states 'At the end of this procedure the board will make its final decision'. For the NUM to accept this document in its entirety would have been a complete surrender. (See Appendix)

It had taken Willis half-a-dozen meetings with MacGregor over a period of two weeks to produce such a document – which amounted to a total betrayal of the striking miners. The NUM tried to amend the document but the NCB said it was 'non-negotiable'. Willis was undeterred. On Tuesday 19 February he and six other trade union leaders achieved their longstanding aim to get back into 10 Downing Street to talk with Thatcher. They told Thatcher and Walker that the NUM was prepared to make concessions and, on the basis of this, an amended document was drawn up and presented to the NUM EC as the 'final word' which was not negotiable. The NUM EC rejected this out of hand. It was said by Arthur Scargill to be '100% worse' than the previous document. Willis pleaded with the NUM EC that the document – which spelt out in even more precise detail the terms for surrender – was 'the best they could get' and had been hammered out at the

90

highest possible level with the Prime Minister in Downing Street. The miners had been betrayed. The consequences were to be disastrous for the NUM.

The TUC had given the government a vital lever to further isolate Arthur Scargill and the striking miners. For now the government could justify its refusal to negotiate on the grounds that the NUM had been totally unreasonable in rejecting what Peter Walker and the NCB called the 'TUC document'. The TUC had done its dirty work. Of all the weapons in Thatcher's arsenal the TUC proved to be the decisive one.

RETURN TO WORK ACCELERATES

During February a steady flow of miners were forced back to work through the financial hardship and cold imposed on their families. After the NUM delegate conference had overwhelmingly rejected the 'TUC document' on 21 February, and further negotiations had been ruled out by the government, the next day showed the highest return to work on any Friday since the beginning of the strike. The following week proved to be the watershed as the NCB claimed a return of 9,455 and that 50 per cent of miners were now working. While the NUM disputed these figures and stated that nearly 60 per cent of miners were still out – representing over 75 per cent of those originally on strike – there could be no denying the significance of this return to work. Yorkshire saw more of its membership back at work in the five days to 1 March than in the previous five weeks.

Very quickly miners' leaders called for a national return to work without an agreement as a way of holding the union together. A delegate conference was called for 3 March to decide on the way forward. On Friday 1 March, Durham, Lancashire, South Wales area councils and the clerical workers, COSA, voted for a national return to work without an agreement. Scotland added a rider that

Free Terry French

250 demonstrators, including miners from Kent, Wales and Notts, defied police threats of arrest to stand cheering and singing as hands appeared through the cell bars of Wandsworth Prison where Terry French, Betteshanger NUM leader, is imprisoned after being given a ferocious five year sentence.

Extracts from Terry French's message to picket:

'We all know why myself and all the other miners have been imprisoned by Thatcher's puppets in the Judiciary, it's because we pose a threat to the cancerous dictatorship she wishes to impose on the working class of this country, but beaten she can be and beaten she will be. I am being treated no differently than the other prisoners except for a few remarks by the odd Tory officer. I am concerned however about the sanitation here. Two toilets, one hot water tap for 58 prisoners on my landing. All washing of eating utensils and personal washing is done in your cell. You are allowed two letters to be sent out each week, one of which you must buy from your earnings of about £1.50 per week. I have already had a final warning about the mail I am receiving (keep sending it). This is Thatcher's Britain 1985.'

TERRY FRENCH

the NUM should return only if a general amnesty was granted for the more than 700 miners sacked for 'offences' directly related to the strike. Eight out of thirteen members of the Midlothian Strike Committee in Scotland have been sacked. Yorkshire area council voted 42-22 to continue the strike. However the council was recalled for Saturday 2 March to give time for delegates to consult their members at branch meetings throughout Yorkshire. The recalled conference voted narrowly (4 votes) to continue the strike. Kent area council also voted against a return without a negotiated settlement. The 3 March delegate conference narrowly voted to go back.The pressures which built up against areas which wished to continue the strike proved too great.

A DIVIDED WORKING CLASS

At a meeting in Castleford, West Yorkshire on 26 February, Arthur Scargill attacked the trade unionists who had failed to come to the assistance of the NUM:

'When history comes to examine this dispute there will be a glaring omission – the fact that trade unionists have been standing on the

'The trade union movement in Britain, with a few notable exceptions, have left this union isolated ... to their eternal shame.' Arthur Scargill, announcing the end of the strike, 3 March 1985

Photo: Norman Willis Number 1 scab

sidelines while this union has been battered by government, Coal Board, police and the whole media propaganda campaign'.

He also emphasised that the level of international support 'from both East and West' had been tremendous, in contrast to Britain where the TUC had failed even to impose a 50p levy on its members. Many members of the NUR and ASLEF refused to move coal throughout the dispute – resulting in the movement of only 200,000 out of the normal 600,000 to 700,000 tonnes a week. Similarly National Union of Seamen members defied management pressure and even legal action in the case of some ships in the North East, in solidarity. But despite their principled stand, coal continued to be mined – by scab miners – and moved – by scab lorry drivers. Steel production continued at almost full rate and – most damaging of all to the striking miners – the power workers, with only a few sporadic exceptions, continued to allow the production of electricity using scab coal and oil.

On Sunday 24 February, over 11 months after the start of the miners' strike, 50,000 miners, their supporters and trade unionists took to the streets of London to demonstrate their support for the strike. It took almost one year, at a time when the miners and their communities had their backs against the wall, for the British Communist Party, through the Liaison Committee for the Defence of Trade Unions, to organise its allies on the 'left' of the trade union bureaucracy for action on the streets of London. And it took place on a Sunday when most of those streets are deserted and when the least sacrifice is demanded from trade union members. At the rally in Trafalgar Square, Arthur Scargill put into perspective nearly 12 months of hard-fought struggle:

London demonstration 24 February 1985

> 'The strike has brought a new dimension to British politics with hundreds of thousands of people involved in support groups not only in this country, but all over the world . . .
>
> We have already achieved a magnificent victory by showing that working people are not prepared to lie down under this Thatcher government. Stand firm. Lift your hearts and eyes to a new horizon and towards saving this industry and our jobs . . .'

Even while Scargill spoke, the forces were at work that have inflicted so much brutality on the mining communities – Thatcher's riot police. 1,000 police, among them mounted police, were hidden off Whitehall and, after an incident had been provoked by them, they came out to attack the last half of the march. Women and children were caught under horses' hooves and even TV cameras later that day showed the sight of an elderly woman being attacked by police and one demonstrator being batoned to the ground. The actions of the police made perfectly clear that *anyone* who supports the miners is a legitimate target for brutality.

Police attack marchers

The demonstration in London on 24 February was an exceptional event due largely to the number of miners and their families present. In contrast the Day of Action 'organised' by the South East Region of the TUC on Monday 11 February was a pathetic affair. Having declared a Day of Action, they then proceeded to say that they had not asked people to take strike action! Consequently the mass picket of Neasden power station numbered only a few hundred, and the picket of Price Waterhouse – the accountants who have carried out the legal theft of NUM funds – numbered less than 100. The Yorkshire and Humberside Day of Action called on the same day was unable to mobilise significant forces.

In the mining areas, particularly in Yorkshire and Scotland, a number of mass pickets took place during February and picketing continued at a basic level at most pits. It is significant that on the day **High Court** (13 February) that a High Court judge outlawed mass picketing at 11 **outlaws mass** Yorkshire pits and forbade the Yorkshire NUM to spend any money **pickets in** on mass pickets, coal was moved for the first time from the key Gas-**Yorkshire** coigne Wood pit in North Yorkshire and from two other Yorkshire pits – Silverwood and Thurcroft. While the injunction did not specifically cover these 3 pits, the NCB was now clearly determined to begin to move coal from the pit heads in Yorkshire. And, as throughout the dispute, the courts paved the way. The Yorkshire NUM EC agreed to abide by the ruling, pending a challenge by South Wales NUM over a similar ruling. Picketing continued in Yorkshire – even at most of the 11 pits covered by the ban. A further major blow to the striking miners was the decision by the Notts miners on 25 February to end the 16 months long overtime ban.

9,542 miners had been arrested in England and Wales up to 15 February, and 7,785 charged up to 26 February. In Scotland a further 1,471 had been arrested up to 1 February. Mass arrests and charges have been used to intimidate miners. On 26 February 23 out of the 87 miners arrested at Harworth colliery in August had charges against them dropped. This is expected to happen with all but 8 of the 87 miners. Their solicitor said this was 'unprecedented' in the case of such serious charges and the miners are sueing the Chief Constable of Notts for wrongful arrest and false imprisonment.

While pickets, marches and rallies continued, primarily in the mining areas, little was done to draw on the powerful potential allies outside the mining areas. Only a massive campaign on the streets of the towns and cities could have provided the momentum to challenge the Thatcher government. The fighting force of these ordinary people, the unemployed, the black and white youth, low paid workers – especially women who have every interest in seeing Thatcher defeated – remained unorganised during the miners' strike. This lack of movement in support of the strike finally allowed opportunists like Willis and Co to step in and do their dirty work – something they had been trying to achieve all along.

BUILDING FOR THE FUTURE

The organised labour movement did not come to the aid of the miners in any decisive way. There was no significant pressure on trade union leaders to carry out their promises and their reactionary stranglehold on the working class movement has continued. Yet there has been no effective challenge to the opportunism of the Labour Party and TUC

leaders from within the miners' ranks. While thousands of miners have come to hate and detest these traitors and while Arthur Scargill has appealed over the heads of the trade union leaders to the rank-and-file and has consistently defended pickets' rights to use violence to defend themselves – against Kinnock's and Willis' criticisms – no organised political challenge to opportunism has emerged.

The total ineffectiveness of the British left means that there is no organised revolutionary current among the miners or in the working class as a whole. The miners' strike, however, has produced a deep crisis in the ranks of the left.

The British left has without exception ignored the split in the working class which has deepened during the strike. Like the Labour Party, the British left is based on the more privileged sections of the working class, and, more importantly, its politics are directed towards the relatively privileged layers of the organised labour movement. Because of this the left does not and has never recognised the revolutionary role of the most oppressed sections of the working class. As the RCG alone argued would happen, right from the start of the strike, miners have come to see new allies among the most oppressed sections of the working class, in those fighting for freedom in the Six Counties of Ireland, and in black people fighting here against the racist British state. This, one of the major political gains of the strike, has completely passed the British left by.

The CPGB has refused to break its links with the Labour Party and TUC bureaucracy. With its internal crisis coming to a head during the

Photo: Police attack demonstration of miners and supporters in Whitehall, London, 24 February 1985 Andrew Wiard/ Report

The British left and the miners' strike

strike, the CPGB has been forced to cover up the TUC's scabbing on the strike – covering up the most basic split in the working class. The *day after* the TUC had said it couldn't contemplate breaking the law to help the miners, the *Morning Star* (7 December 1984) headline read 'TUC pledges "we will keep NUM going"'.

The SWP, like most of the Trotskyist left, sees only a split between the rotten bureaucracy and the fighting rank-and-file. Because of this they can only explain the inability of the miners to win an outright victory by blaming firstly the Labour Party and trade union bureaucracy, and secondly the leadership of the NUM and, in the last few months, Arthur Scargill himself.

So the scabbing of the majority of Notts miners is put down to the wrong picketing tactics of the NUM leadership and the failure of the great majority of the organised labour movement to support the miners is attributed to 'right wing union leaders'. Chris Harman tells us, in an SWP pamphlet *The miners strike and the struggle for socialism*, that:

> 'The enthusiasm for solidarity from rank-and-file activists has not been matched by the official leaders' (page 10)

This simplistic division is easily destroyed by a cursory examination of the actual positions taken by many rank-and-file dockers, electricians, power workers, steel workers, and transport workers, especially the lorry drivers. The fact that many railway workers and seamen have given active solidarity to the strike only highlights the overall betrayals throughout the organised working class movement. A point which might escape Harman but which thousands of striking miners fully understand.

The TUC and Labour Party has scabbed on the strike not simply because its leaders are rotten and well off but because the movement itself represents the interests of the more privileged layers of the working class. It is their movement.

Refusing to recognise this, the British left in the last few months of the strike, with the pressures on the mining communities to abandon the strike becoming more intense, saw fit to attack Arthur Scargill – the most outstanding and principled trade union leader in Britain for decades. The SWP, for example, attacked Scargill for not speaking out openly 'about the lethargy, the incompetence and bureaucratic sabotage of so many of the officials under him'. They said his silence was 'almost criminal'.

At the very moment when the ruling class was intent on isolating Arthur Scargill as an unrepresentative 'extremist', the left wants him to purge his own officials. Scargill, unlike the left, has troops to lead and has to deal with political reality and the real balance of forces within the miners' strike. The NUM is not a revolutionary organisation, but a trade union with all the political limitations which that entails. Arthur Scargill cannot change this and neither can the SWP.

Some six months before the miners' strike began, the RCG, in its manifesto, *The revolutionary road to communism in Britain* stated:

'...a revolutionary trend cannot arise or be built first and

96

foremost in the existing Labour Party and trade union movement. This does not rule out the development of massive working class struggles as rank-and-file trade unionists are forced out of desperate necessity to defend jobs, wages and living standards. Only that such workers and their struggles will inevitably be betrayed by the very same leaders who have consistently betrayed the Irish people, the black people and all peoples oppressed by British imperialism.'

The miners' strike has confirmed this, but a year of bitter struggle has thrown up new class organisations that can take the struggle of the working class forward. We have seen this in the work of the women's support groups in the mining areas and the miners support groups in the towns and cities – organisations outside the control of the Labour and trade union bureaucracies. The resistance of the mining communities has indeed 'brought a new dimension to British politics'.

The miners' struggle will go on even with the miners back at work. Resistance to NCB management, bent on attacking the more militant miners, will be necessary. The more than 700 miners victimised and sacked for fighting for their class have to be defended and reinstated in their jobs. The more than 150 class war prisoners, the most resolute class fighters among the miners, must likewise be defended and their struggle for political rights in prison centrally taken up in the movement outside. Material and financial support must be organised by the NUM and the support groups for the victimised miners and their families until they are reinstated, and for the imprisoned miners and their families. If all this is done and the political gains of the strike are consolidated and its political lessons learned, then history will confirm that the miners' strike 1984/5 was a turning point in the struggle of the British working class.

2-3 March 1985

TUC-NCB document

The text of TUC/NCB document put to executives of the NUM and NACODS, 15 February 1985.

1. It is of crucial importance for the parties concerned in the current dispute to concentrate attention on the future success of the industry and in so doing to commit themselves to a reconciliation and restoration of relationships.

2. The NUM recognise that it is the duty of the NCB to manage the industry efficiently, and to secure sound developments in accordance with their responsibilities and the NCB recognise that the NUM represents and advances the interests of its members and their employment opportunities. In this regard the NCB is firmly of the view that the interests of the membership of the NUM are best served by the development of an economically sound industry.

3. The parties undertake that immediately upon a return to normal working discussions will commence upon the revision of the plan for Coal such revision to be completed within six months. In order that this programme which is of vital importance to the industry, the mining communities and the country is carried through with utmost effectiveness, the parties specifically and mutually commit themselves to giving maximum priority to this period of conciliation and reconstruction and providing the necessary resources. The TUC undertake to give assistance if called on by either the NUM or the NCB. The issues that could be included in discussions are attached as an annex. Nothing in this paragraph will prevent any party from referring collieries to the review procedure.

4. The parties accept that it is of value to outline, at this stage, the procedures that flow from a commitment to modify the Colliery Review Procedure.

5. The existing Colliery Review Procedure has the objective of periodically reviewing at colliery and area level the performance and future investment opportunities of pits with representatives of unions. The parties accept the need to modify the procedure. After a return to normal working there will be urgent talks about the early establish-

ment of modified procedure and about the constitution, membership and role of the independent reference body which is to be incorporated into the procedure. Until such time existing procedures will apply.

6. Proposals about the future of pits will then be dealt with through the modified Colliery Review Procedure in accordance with past practices, those pits which are exhausted or facing severe geological difficulties will be closed by joint agreement and in the case of a colliery where there are no further reserves which can be developed to provide the board in line with their responsibilities with a satisfactory basis for continuing operations such a colliery will be closed.

7. Under the modified Colliery Review Procedure the independent body will constitute a further consultative stage after the national appeal stage to consider reference from any of the parties to the procedure where agreement is not reached in the usual steps at colliery and area level. All parties are committed to give full weight to the views of the proposed independent review body.

8. At the end of this procedure, the board will make its final decision. The parties accept this is not intended to constitute a no strike agreement.

Imperialism versus the miners: 'A little local difficulty'

The ruling class press screams in horror at meetings between representatives of the National Union of Mineworkers (NUM) and the governments of the socialist countries and Libya. Yet they are mute on the links between Thatcher, MacGregor and transnational corporations and banks which they serve. The alliance of banking capital, giant industrial combines and the state stands at the heart of imperialism. In the oil industry we can see condensed the trends of world trade and capitalism. Today, the banks and transnationals are collaborating to tighten their hold on the world's energy supplies and distribution. Their use of the British state against the NUM and for the control and destruction of the British coal industry are part of this strategy. By fighting for their jobs British miners have joined the frontline of those resisting the global plans of imperialism.

MACGREGOR: 'FORTY FIVE YEARS ON THE LABOUR FRONT'

'I am not one of your local characters. I vote in Florida'. So spoke National Coal Board Chairman, Ian MacGregor, who went on to describe the miners' strike as 'a little local difficulty'. Indeed, MacGregor's interests and horizons stretch far beyond the British coalfields; his casual arrogance bears the hallmark of one of capitalism's men of the world: a doyen of high finance, whose trade binds the globe with a million lines of credit.

MacGregor was appointed Deputy Chairman of British Leyland in 1977 by the Labour Secretary of State for Industry, Eric Varley, who made the South African Michael Edwardes, Chairman at the same time. In 1980 Keith Joseph persuaded Mac-

Gregor to take on the chair of the British Steel Corporation (BSC). The New York based merchant bank Lazard Frères, of which MacGregor is a partner and thus part owner, were paid £675,000 plus a 'performance related' bonus of up to £1,150,000 for his services. By 1981 Thatcher had grown pleased with her acquisition, describing MacGregor as 'the best politician in Britain' and offering Lazards a further $1.8m bonus if he could get the steel industry to 'break even' in two years. BSC employed 166,000 workers in 1980; by the end of 1983 there were 80,000. Mac-Gregor contemptuously dismissed steel

> 'The Thatcher government is merely an executive committee, one of many, of the giant corporations who now control the resources of the so-called free world and isn't that phrase an insult to the intelligence of the people in that so-called free world! In our own situation we are opposed not just to the government, we are opposed to those big international monopolies such as BP, Esso, Arco, all these giant companies which in fact now have a long term strategy to buy up the coal, oil and gas reserves of the world so that they can play their game with the price of energy which everyone needs. And that is the long term strategy behind this strike. The present government is being urged forward by their masters in the boardrooms of international capitalism to break the back of the miners' union, and also the organisations of the entire working class...'
>
> Malcolm Pitt, President Kent NUM at the Irish Solidarity Movement Conference, October 14, 1984.

> **'Transnationals produce and distribute an increasingly important share of all the goods in the world capitalist system and generate the biggest share of international capital flow which they control by means of a vast international financial network. This means that these international monopolies are the principal agents in the world capitalist process of accumulation and exploitation. This has naturally had great social and political effects for Third World countries.'**
> **President Fidel Castro.**

union leader Bill Sirs, '... In forty five years on the labour front it was the most poorly judged position I've seen.'

Before being invited to join Lazards in 1978 MacGregor had distinguished himself as Chairman of the US transnational corporation Amax. He had led the company since the 1960s and was Honorary Chairman up to 1982. Formerly American Metal Climax, Amax is the third largest US coal company, it trades minerals and petroleum out of fourteen countries with a concentration of investments in Southern Africa. In 1975 MacGregor had a personal investment of $2m in Amax and Standard Oil of California (now Chevron) bought up twenty per cent of the company. It began investing heavily in oil in the Gulf of Mexico, the North Sea and Western Australia. However, it is the Southern African investments that flourished best under MacGregor.

Amax bought up twenty nine per cent of the Tsumeb copper mining complex in Namibia, which was accused by the International Commission of Jurists of running a contract labour system 'akin to slavery'. In Northern Rhodesia, now Zambia, Amax collaborated with the Anglo-American Corporation to exploit its copper deposits. Accumulated profits were used to invest in South Africa itself, where mining wages were held down to about a sixth of the average US miner's wage. Amax's South African investments are intertwined with British and South African capital. For his

contributions towards the systematic looting of the oppressed southern African people MacGregor was awarded an Honorary Doctorate of Science at the University of Angola in 1970, by the fascist Portuguese colonial rulers, and in 1978 he won the Rand Gold Medal of the American Institute of Mining, Metallurgy and Petroleum Engineers for his contribution to South African mining.

The methods used to extract profit from African labour were then turned by Mac-Gregor upon the US miners. In 1974 Amax refused to sign a contract with the United Mineworkers of America which would ensure union members limited benefits concerning pensions, medical assistance for disabled miners, and a say in the safety conditions in the mines. Miners at the Belle Ayre colliery in Wyoming struck in January 1975, other collieries worked to rule in sympathy. Chevron moved in with its bid. The union complained to the Federal Trade Commission that this was a move to finance union busting activities. Amax threatened strikers with dismissal and posted advice to union members on how they could resign from the union and strike-break without penalty. MacGregor harnessed the law and ancilliary gangs to crush the miners as they had been dealt with in Southern Africa. He wheeled in the popular Country and Western singer Loretta Lynn to sing out the praises of Amax. By March 1975 production at the Belle Ayre pit had recommenced, and although miners picketed it for a further two years the strike was lost. A combination of brute force, the law, insidious propaganda and big financial backing won, leading the way to a current US coal industry which is sixty per cent non-unionised, and over sixty per cent owned by the oil transnationals.

Tory preparations for an assault upon the British miners had been under way since the defeats dealt the Conservative government in 1972 and 1974. According to the *Financial Times* it was Frank Chapple, former electricians' and power workers' union leader, who suggested that MacGregor should be appointed to head the NCB, because 'it was essential to find someone who was not going to be frightened of Arthur Scargill'. Thatcher needed little encouragement. With MacGregor's appointment in September 1983 the merchant banker was promised £1,150,000 if he achieved on the British coalfields what he had in the rusting steel mills, the non-unionised mines of the USA, and the oppressed nations of Southern Africa and South Africa itself.

SCOUTING FOR CAPITAL

'A monopoly, once it is formed and controls thousands of millions, inevitably penetrates into every sphere of public life, regardless of the form of government and all other "details".'

V Lenin, *Imperialism The Highest Stage of Capitalism*

Only the most cunning and ruthless capitalists are invited into the ranks of the merchant bankers. Among their functions are to serve as scouts for large scale capital: reconnoitering markets, company accounts and share prices, analysing them and selecting targets for purchase. When the target company is located the merchant bank will arrange lines of credit, for a fee, for the giants of the capitalist world to make their bids with. By these means the weaker capitalists are devoured by the stronger, and capital is directed towards its most profitable grounds. Merchant bankers are in the vanguard of capital, and they themselves are in a position to take large holdings in the companies they form. Lazard's directors sit on the boards of over sixty US corporations. It gained the reputation of being 'the merger bank'; arranging the RCA takeover of Random House and Hertz, the McDonnell Corporation takeover of Douglas Aircraft Company (the conglomerate manufactures jet-fighters for the US and Israeli forces), Fiat's merger with Citroen, and many more. The most infamous of Lazard's creations is the US electronic giant ITT, which was proven to have helped destabilise the Popular Unity government in Chile, and which President Allende accused of 'attempting to bring about civil war' in his land. CIA agents sat on the board of ITT, and a year after the bloody military coup in Chile the Director of the CIA, at the time, John McCone, was given a directorship of ITT.

Lazards was founded upon the merchandise of the slave trade in 1847, selling drapery out of New Orleans. In 1848 it moved to San Francisco, dealing gold out of New York and establishing banking houses in Paris and London. The gold led Lazards into the heart of the British banking system and the ruling class. It provided the basis for credits which helped establish colonial rule across Africa and Asia. Lazards invested in Anglo-Dutch oil interests. The British section of Lazards is interwoven through share-ownership with the US company. Lazard Brothers in Britain is largely owned by the Pearson group, which is a major shareholder of Shell and maintains oil investments in Texas. Lazard's directors include a former chairman of the Conservative Party, the director of the former Reserve Bank of Rhodesia, the Chairman of the Commonwealth Development Corporation, the President of the Anglo-Taiwan Trade Committee etc, etc. Lazards founded the first merchant bank in South Africa along with the Anglo-American Corporation: Union Acceptances in 1955. Lazards led the way in raising loans for the South African government from the London money market in 1970, after this source had been denied the apartheid regime since 1959. Merchant bankers like MacGregor are in the vanguard of imperialism: from boardrooms and jets they plan its strategy, direct the tactics, and wield capital against labour across frontiers.

Karl Marx described how each capitalist crisis accelerated the concentration of ownership of production resources into fewer and fewer hands, and speeded up the exploitation of the workforce in order to keep up the rate of return on investment.

Crises are boom-times for the merchant bankers: it is then that they scale the commanding heights of capital. Crusader for free-enterprise and competition Ronald Reagan has loosened US anti-trust laws to facilitate the concentration process. In Britain last year Lazard Brothers multiplied the value of its merger business five fold upon the 1982 figure. The Pearson group itself includes Lazards, the *Financial Times,* half *The Economist* and *Investors' Chronicle,* Penguin and Viking Books, Madame Tussauds and Royal Doulton. Significantly, such mergers when directed by the most astute merchant banker can bring tasty pickings: Texaco and Shell for instance are reckoned by *The Economist* to be paying $4 a barrel for oil through purchases of other producers and distributors, about a seventh of its market price!

In 1983 the total value of US company mergers was $73.1bn, more than a third again greater than in 1972. The imperialist oil industry saw $15bn worth of mergers in 1983, a half again greater than in 1982. This year the merger market is breaking all records. In the first quarter of 1984 the value of US takeovers was put at over $20bn, twice any previous quarterly record. Significantly, Texaco has bought Getty Oil for $10.2bn, Mobil absorbed Superior Oil for $5.7bn, and Chevron took Gulf for $13.4bn. The rate of concentration in the energy industry has been phenomenal: Conaco, Dupont, Elf Equitaire, Marathon and Phillips Oil are just some of the other

Photo: 'Amax and MacGregor paved the way for mass unemployment on the US coalfields, for families to sell up their possessions, travel and sleep in their cars in the desperate search for work'

corporations that have been gobbling or gobbled up in the recent period: directed by the bankers and strengthening a monopoly hold over energy sources and markets for a handful of multi-millionaires.

THE MANIPULATIONS OF HIGH FINANCE

'There have been more and more banks entering the energy lending field in the past five years . . . The industry is borrowing more and more money all the time.'

James Anderson, Vice-President of Chase Manhattan Bank.

'Capitalists are concerned with profits not what their assets look like. The activities of the banks allow them to obtain an increasing share of the profits produced world-wide even though they, themselves, produce no wealth at all. Money which makes money – capital in its most parasitic form.'

Revolutionary Communist Group Manifesto: *The revolutionary road to communism in Britain.*

Each merger among the transnationals carries a load of new debt. The merchant bank is a busy go-between for the energy transnationals and the banks. Lazard's and MacGregor's New York address is 1, Rockefeller Plaza, top suite above the Rockefeller Centre which directs the Chase Manhattan Bank and the Standard Oil Energy concerns. A quarter of the directors of the Bank of England stem from merchant banks or the oil transnationals. Imperialist banks have put up to 90 per cent of the purchase price for recent oil mergers. They stand to earn vast interest payments and to wield control over a vital commodity. In March alone, the start of the NUM strike, the US magazine *Business Week* noted that the imperialist banks had put aside $34bn as standby loans for merger purposes; that is triple the total requirement for 1983. Atlantic Richfield (Arco) raised $12bn to bid for Gulf, but Chevron outbid them raising $14bn. Nonetheless, Arco will still have to pay $7m in fees to the

bank syndicate, led by Chase Manhattan, for the credit line set up to allow Arco to bid. Merchant banks were paid $63m for their joint efforts in raising funds for the various bidders for Gulf.

The parasitic character of decaying capitalism is displayed in the gains of T Boone Pickens, who personally made fortunes of $43.6m and $31.6m out of speculative share dealings in the midst of two oil merger scrambles. His Mesa petroleum is currently bidding for Phillips Oil. However, it is the banks which best stand to feast upon the profits of mergers, and to expand their economic control and political power. Merchant bankers like MacGregor are their handservants, and it is the working class and oppressed of the world that are served upon their tray.

The huge demand for credit required by the energy transnationals to carry out mergers has contributed to rises in interest rates. Chief victims of this are the oppressed nations, soaked in unpayable debts of over $810bn to the imperialist banks. Each half-per-cent rise in interest rates takes an additional $3.5bn out of the world's poorest nations. Four successive interest rate rises on the US money markets in Spring 1984, coinciding with giant mergers, added $13bn to the oppressed nations' debts! Out of Latin America alone they added an extra $3.5bn to debt repayments, only just under $1bn less than the continent spends on food imports for its people, a third of whom rot in hunger. Each year the parasitic transnationals whom MacGregor serves plunder between $150bn and $200bn from the oppressed nations. This, combined with the debt burden which will take, for example, a third of Latin America's export earnings in repayments this year, prevents the oppressed nations from developing their own energy resources, forces them into increasing dependence upon the likes of Amax, the British banks and the energy transnationals.

Through the process of concentration oil companies now form twelve of the world's twenty biggest transnationals.

Between them they control over seventy five per cent of capitalism's trade in petroleum. This degree of monopolisation allows them to manipulate market prices for maximum profitability. Between 1973 and 1982 oil prices increased ten fold, about three times the average for world commodity prices, and more than tripled the oppressed nations' expenditure on oil imports, absorbing over a quarter of their export earnings.

In 1982 any sugar exporting country had to produce and sell nine times as much in order to buy a ton of oil as in 1960. The imperialist banks conspire with the energy transnationals to keep oil prices high: they fear that a steep decline in oil prices will mean that their big clients like Mexico, Indonesia and Nigeria, oil producers, will be unable to repay their loans and interest. Not surprisingly, just seven of the oil transnationals made combined profits of over $24bn in 1980.

The imperialist banks, the transnationals and the imperialist states are directly responsible for mass hunger in the world. In keeping with their trade of preying upon the weak, Lazard Frères have developed a new enterprise; as financial advisers to the tyrannies of Turkey, Sri Lanka, Indonesia, Panama and Zaire among others. Helping to arrange the conditions of the masses so that they become 'economically viable' through the bloody repression of state forces, so that the imperialist banks will profit from the mountains of debt heaped upon the oppressed. Wherever these jet-borne parasites like MacGregor descend they and their local henchmen meet resistance on the streets!

IMPERIALIST PLANS FOR COAL

'The intensity of competition between fuels will make it important for companies to consider setting a foot in more than one camp ... In the future, increasing attention may be paid to their access to diverse types of energy.'
First National City Bank, Energy Memo 1967.

With the imperialist crisis deepening in the 1970s and 80s the growth in demand for energy has slowed. World oil consumption fell nearly 8 per cent over 1979-80. This slowing has put pressure on oil prices to fall and accelerated the merger process to counter its effects at the same time. The transnationals have sought to dominate the potential rival coal industry, and have led opposition to the Soviet gas pipeline link with western Europe. With its sights set on the imminent British miners' strike, Shell lobbied in London and Washington for increased British coal imports. The mammoth banking and transnational investments in oil require energy market domination if profits are to be realised and the banks repaid.

Proven imperialist oil reserves are estimated at forty years supply while coal reserves would last two hundred years. Even though, on average, coal is 55 to 65 per cent cheaper than fuel oil for industrial uses coal production in the US, Canada and Australia, containing three quarters of imperialism's coal deposits, is being run at 20 per cent below capacity. With their huge profits such as Exxon, BP, Shell and Chevron have bought up mines and begun diversification into nuclear and other forms of energy. Over sixty per cent of US coal reserves are owned by the oil transnationals. With the criminal logic of the market place three thousand US mines, half the total, have been shut down in the last six years. US mines are deserted as soon as they are dug! The Pennsylvania, West Virginia and Kentucky coalfields are running at 40 per cent of their capacity. Amax and MacGregor paved the way for mass unemployment on the US coalfields, for families to sell up their possessions, travel and sleep in their cars in the desperate search for work. This is what MacGregor means when he preached from a City of London pulpit: 'Miners are an international breed. The important thing about mining communities is their mobility.' As a merchant banker MacGregor directs capital towards its most fertile feeding grounds. Exceptionally, South Africa is increasing its coal production and trade: jetties are under construction and by 1987 South Africa, with the assistance of Amax and Anglo-American, intends to increase its coal exports from 30 million to 44 million tonnes, a quarter of world trade in coal.

MacGregor will be satisfied only when conditions on the British coalfields approach those in Southern Africa, then, with a huge reserve army of unemployed labour and broken unions, 'privatisation' could begin. The transnationals would move in, their hired hand having paved the way.

MINERS, OPPRESSED AND REVOLUTIONARY PEOPLES UNITE

'The Vietnamese Miners' Trade Union has been closely following and whole-heartedly supporting the heroic struggle waged by the British miners to defend their right to work, their social welfare achievements, and the freedom of trade unionism'.
Press release, Embassy of the Socialist Republic of Vietnam, London.

The British miners have faced the same concentration of ownership and distribution, the same manipulation of markets that confronts the oppressed masses of

Asia, Africa and Latin America. They have experienced something of the techniques of violent repression and cynical manipulation of the law that is meted out to the oppressed, be they in South Africa, Chile or Ireland. Thatcher and MacGregor personify the vulgar brutality of imperialism: that alliance of banking capital, transnationals and the state. Its strength has been drawn from generations of poor and oppressed people across the globe. British oil consumption between August and October rose 40.6 per cent on last year's figures for the same months: additional imports of half a million barrels a day. Phillips and Drew, London stockbrokers, estimate that Britain is paying £250-300 million a month in extra oil costs to provide fuel for power plants to keep running and exhaust the miners' determination. The money to pay for this is wrung from the poor and oppressed of Britain by the British state and is choked out of the masses of the world by the banks and transnationals.

Labour aristocrats like Varley, Sirs, Chapple and Kinnock are inheritors of a long line of treachery bought by imperialist super-profits. They recognise the threat posed to them and their privileges by unity between British workers in struggle, the world's oppressed masses and the socialist and anti-imperialist countries. They will do all in their power to prevent the emergence of such unity, but that unity is the only way forward, the only way to weaken the imperialist ruling class.

At a recent meeting of the Wall Street Stock Exchange, a training ground for MacGregor 'skills', CIA Director William Casey described the oppressed nations as the 'principal battleground' for imperialism and the transnationals as 'the most effective means' of achieving victory. Thatcher, MacGregor and the British state have brought the battleground into the heartland of imperialism. The British miners' struggle is saluted by oppressed and revolutionary peoples across the globe.

TREVOR RAYNE

PUBLIC WARNING
Belfast today –
Orgreave tomorrow
Ban Plastic Bullets

Speech made at a Fitzwilliam public meeting 10 October 1984

It's an honour and privilege for me to speak to striking miners, their families and supporters. It is a measure of the political impact of the miners' strike – how it has roused the political consciousness of hundreds of thousands of people – that the issue of Ireland is now being raised so widely.

On the one hand your direct experience of repression at the hands of the police, the courts and the law has led many miners and their supporters to start asking what the connection is between the repression you are facing and the repression the Irish people have faced for 15 years now.

On the other hand the ruling class has seen in your courage and determination a threat to its privilege and power, just as the courageous and determined struggle of the Nationalist people in Ireland has threatened that same privilege and power.

In the course of this strike for the basic right to a job you have refused to allow your struggle to be limited by the legal and constitutional rules laid down by the Thatcher government . . . or by the narrow self interest of better off layers of the working class – some in your own ranks – their organisations or political parties.

Arthur Scargill expresses this position directly when he says he would rather go to prison than betray his class.

'I stand by my class, by my union – and if that means prison so be it. We have come too far, we have suffered too much for there to be any compromise with either the judiciary or the government.'

In the eyes of the ruling class for miners to stand by their class is a *crime* – for it directly challenges the power of the wealthy and privileged who rule this society.

Hence the force of the state, its police, its courts, its laws and its prisons are being used against you.

It is no surprise therefore that the ruling class should speak openly about the possibility of using plastic bullets against picketers.

Eldon Griffiths, Tory MP, official parliamentary spokesman for the Police Federation, stated at the end of September,

'Police will soon need to be equipped with plastic bullets to combat armed pickets firing air guns and other weapons.'

The plastic bullet is a lethal weapon designed to murder and maim unarmed civilians. David Kitson – South African political prisoner recently released after a 20 year sentence – said of the firing of plastic bullets at young blacks in South Africa,

'The South Africans are learning from the British "how to murder people in a civilised way"'.

Rubber and plastic bullets have been used against Nationalist demonstrators in the Six Counties of Ireland since 1970 and for the same reason as they have been prepared for use against you.

The struggle of the Nationalist minority in the Six Counties of Ireland began as did your struggle, peacefully. They marched against sectarian discrimination and for fundamental democratic rights. They were

107

batoned off the street by the police – the Royal Ulster Constabulary (RUC). They were brutalised, shot at and their houses were burnt out. On 14 August 1969 nine year old Patrick Rooney had half his head blown away by high velocity bullets fired by the RUC, which pierced the wall of his bedroom and killed him in his bed. This was before the Provisional IRA existed.

This brutal repression failed to drive the Nationalist minority into submission. They organised mass protests and demonstrations against the paramilitary forces of the Six Counties statelet – and against the British army that was sent in by a Labour government to prop up the sectarian loyalist statelet.

Rubber bullets, the precedessor of plastic bullets, were first fired in 1970 as one means of controlling the Nationalist population and driving them off the street. They were used as an alternative to the widely condemned CS gas and the unwieldy water cannon.

Statistics for the number of rubber and, later, plastic bullets fired show conclusively that these weapons are used to break up demonstrations and other forms of mass street protest.

In the five years from 1970-75, 59,648 rubber and plastic bullets were fired. 52,881 (88%) were fired in 1971/2/3 – the peak of demonstrations and protests against internment (August 1971) and Bloody Sunday (January 1972).

In the four years from 1976 to 1980, 9,190 plastic bullets were fired; however in eleven months in 1981 29,665 plastic bullets were fired, 16,666 in May alone. This was of course the period of the hunger strike and the associated demonstrations and protests. Bobby Sands died on 5 May 1981 after enduring 66 days on hunger strike. Fifteen people have been killed by plastic/rubber bullets from 1972 to 1984; 7 of the fifteen people killed were killed in 1981. 7 of those killed were children.

Riot control (anti-civilian) weapons are being introduced in Britain and will be used in the same way as they have been in Ireland: to break up and attack demonstrations and other forms of public protest.

During the uprisings of black and white youth in British cities in 1981, CS gas was used in Liverpool 8. CS grenades designed to penetrate walls were fired at people causing serious injuries. During the miners' strike it has been confirmed that police forces have in the region of 20,000 plastic bullets stocked in Britain.

It is clear that the purpose of the plastic bullet is to break up mass protests by terror. From 1970-72 the Royal Victoria Hospital in Belfast carried out a survey of 90 patients hit by rubber bullets; 80% of these had head injuries. All of the 15 people killed by rubber and plastic bullets in Ireland were hit above the waist.

(The rules for the use of plastic bullets say that they must not be fired at a distance less than 20 metres, unless there is a serious threat to the safety of officers and others. They should be aimed below the waist, and they must be fired at selected people, not indiscriminately into a crowd.)

The recent events on 12 August this year where a peaceful demonstration was attacked in West Belfast, and one man, John Downes, was murdered with scores badly injured, demonstrates that the rules are as meaningless as the rules covering police violence against miners' pickets. John Downes was shot at a range of 2 metres in the chest and the RUC put out a whole series of lies to explain away the brutality and murder.

It should be remembered that plastic bullets are not an alternative to lead bullets. They are used in addition to them. In January 1972, Bloody Sunday, 14 peaceful demonstrators were shot dead in cold blood by the British army. In the last two years at least 19 Nationalists have been killed in shoot-to-kill operations by the RUC and the British army.

The same kind of treatment meted out to the Irish will be used against the British working class for the same reason as the miners' strike has dramatically shown.

If the Social and Democratic Labour Party – the 'moderate' constitutional nationalist party – could control the fight back of the Nationalist people in the Six Counties of Ireland, there would be no plastic bullets being fired in Ireland because there would be no effective threat to the wealth and privilege of the British ruling class.

Just as if the Kinnocks, Murrays, the Bill Sirs and the scab miners could control your fight back there would be no threat of plastic bullets being used against you.

For you and for the Irish people the message from the British ruling class is the same. You may protest only so long as your protest poses no serious threat. You may picket so long as your picketing is ineffective. However, as soon as you decide that your rights – in the case of the miners the right to a job; in the case of the Irish people the right to self-determination – are to be fought for effectively then the rules of engagement will quickly change.

The law, as General Sir Frank Kitson, head of the UK Land Forces, said in his book *Low Intensity Operations, subversion, insurgency and peace keeping,* is:

'just another weapon in the government's arsenal and it becomes little more than a propaganda cover for the disposal of unwanted members of the public . . .'

The law, the media and the courts will be manipulated to render your struggle, again as has happened with the Irish struggle, a criminal struggle. In Ireland a whole array of special legislation exists to make the struggle of the Nationalist people a crime and give the RUC and British army virtually unlimited power to arrest and detain.

People are arrested under the Emer-

Photo: John Downes murdered, Belfast 12 August 1984 Derek Speirs/Report

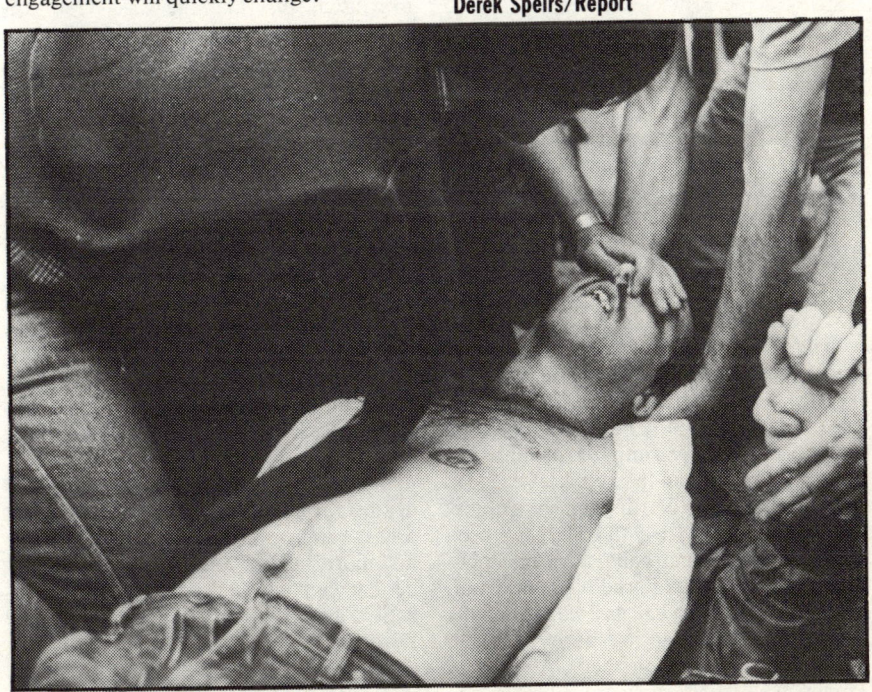

gency Powers Act and/or the Prevention of Terrorism Act. They can be held for years on remand before their case comes to court. People are then convicted in specially created non-jury courts by loyalist judges. From 1976 to 1979 torture was used to extract confessions out of suspects before they were taken to court. Today paid informers are used to fabricate evidence against Nationalists. 35 people were sentenced to over 4,000 years in prison solely on the statement of a paid and bought-off informer.

Obscure acts like the Flags and Emblems Act 1954, make it an offence to fly the Tricolour – the Irish flag. The Whiterock leisure centre in Nationalist Belfast is threatened with closure because of a Tricolour flying from the roof.

After the Nationalist people followed the constitutional path demanded by the British government and put Bobby Sands up for election, which he won convincingly, the British changed the rules so prisoners could no longer stand in elections. Today the British refuse to talk to elected Sinn Fein representatives.

In Britain the Prevention of Terrorism Act has been used to intimidate Irish people in order to discourage them from political activity in support of the Republican Movement in Ireland.

Of the 5,600 people arrested up to 1983 under the PTA, 86 (1.5%) were found guilty and 104 charged with so-called terrorist offences (1.8%).

Today in Britain, trade union law is being used to criminalise effective picketing including so-called 'secondary' picketing. During the miners' strike, bail conditions have been imposed on miners to prevent them from picketing. Of 1,745 miners charged in Nottinghamshire alone, to 28 September, 1,649 (94.5%) have been granted conditional bail – have had political bail conditions placed on them. In all, 3,839 miners are on bail and we can assume that the vast majority have had bail conditions imposed on them. Already 39 miners have received prison sentences. The

law is being used to remove 'unwanted members' of the NUM from the picket lines.

We have seen the use of archaic laws to arrest people during the miners' strike. The Conspiracy and Protection of property act of 1875 – last used in 1972 against the Shrewsbury building workers, 3 of whom were sent to prison, one for 3 years – is being used against the miners.

James Anderton, Chief Constable of Manchester, makes the position of the ruling class crystal clear. He said mass pickets:

'...were acts of terrorism without the bullet and the bomb'

The use of the term 'terrorist' is no coincidence or mistake. Any force which threatens the power of the ruling class is invariably labelled 'terrorist'.

So the democratic right to protest, to picket, to organise against scabs is being criminalised, just like the struggle of the Nationalist people in Ireland. Kenneth Newman, head of the Metropolitan Police, almost certainly playing an organising role in centralising police activities against the miners, recently made it clear how he would deal with unwelcome protests here in Britain when he said that 'when willing compliance with the law was not present the police had to apply coercion.' When Newman was head of the Royal Ulster Constabulary in the Six Counties of Ireland, that coercion involved the torture of suspects in order to put them away for a very long period of time.

As more laws against working class struggle are enacted, eg the Police and Criminal Evidence Bill – which will legalise many actions now illegal and being used against the miners (road blocks, sealing off areas, raiding homes etc) – so will more and more political and trade union activity be labelled criminal and effective mass action against such laws will be labelled terrorism.

The lessons being learned by many miners today are the same as those under-

110

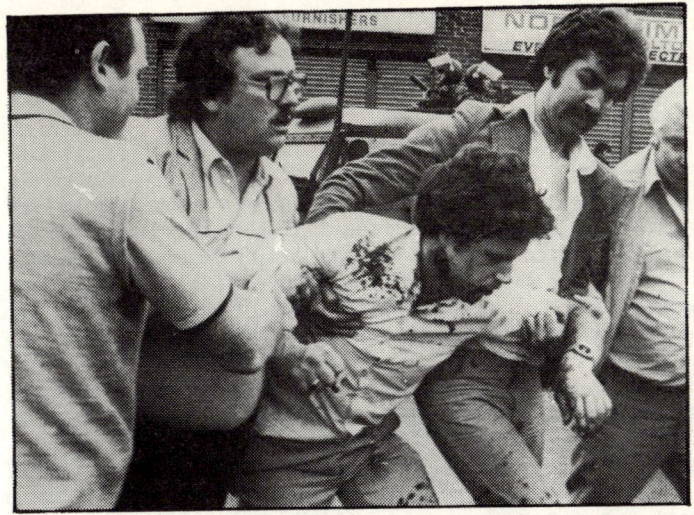

Photo: A man
severely injured
by plastic bullets
helped away by
friends, Belfast
12 August 1984
Paul Mattsson

stood by the Irish people many years ago.

That is, that when the struggle of working people for their rights conflicts with the rule of profit and the dominance of the wealthy, the ruling class will use every means at its disposal – it will disregard its own laws and so-called 'democracy' – to maintain its own power.

The ruling class which has murdered 15 people with plastic bullets in the Six Counties of Ireland, is the same British ruling class which will use plastic bullets against you if they think it necessary . . .

Miners in Britain and the people of Ireland do face a common enemy in the British ruling class. For far too long many British workers have allowed the British ruling class to repress the Irish people, and as a consequence have strengthened the ability of the ruling class to repress British workers. For far too long the leadership of the Labour and trade union movement have been allowed to support British repression against the Irish people. Indeed the Labour Party in power has on each occasion actively extended the repression against the Irish people.

It is no coincidence that this same Labour and trade union leadership today has condemned miners' 'violence' on the picket lines – and in some cases has openly prevented solidarity action with the miners' strike.

As I said in the beginning, your struggle and your direct experience has led to many more people asking the question 'What is the connection between the struggle of the miners for jobs and the struggle of the Irish people for self-determination?'

Karl Marx wrote over 100 years ago,

'a nation which oppresses another can never itself be free'

You should support the Irish people in their struggle for self-determination because it is part of your struggle for your jobs, your communities and your rights against the common enemy of the Irish people and the British working class – the British ruling class.

When we demand the banning of plastic bullets in Britain and Ireland, we are recognising that common enemy.

The Irish people fighting for self-determination are our allies in the struggle to free ourselves from the rule of profit and all the devastation and misery that that rule brings. . . The Irish struggle and your struggle are one struggle, one fight.

DAVID REED

111

The media and the miners' strike

The ruling class lie-machine is a highly developed mechanism which has always been used against the Irish people, black people, trade unionists and anyone else who opposes the rule of profit. During the miners' strike this machine has been brought out once again to lie, distort and censor on behalf of the wealthy minority whose rule is threatened by the courage and determination of striking miners and their communities. What follow are but a few examples of the lie-machine in action.

Every day the media vilify Arthur Scargill. Everything from his hair to his politics has become poison in the pens of ruling class propagandists. The most infamous single attack took place in May when the *Sun* tried to run a front page story under the headline 'Mine Führer' accompanied by a photograph taken in such a way as to make Scargill appear to be giving a Nazi salute. This filth was stopped by *Sun* printworkers who prevented its appearance. The photograph, however, appeared in many papers. The biggest lie of all has been the attempt to portray the strike as the result of Scargill's 'manipulation' of miners. Scargill answered this in August when he said:

'The miners' strike of 1984 did not spring fully grown from the head of one individual (as the capitalist press and indeed television news would have you believe). It was the response of thousands of men and women to a pit closure threat as savage as it was senseless.'

On 22 May *The Guardian, The Times, Daily Telegraph, Daily Express, Sun* and *Standard* published a picture of NUM member Frank Branwell 'returning to work' at Markham colliery. Frank Branwell did not return to work. He spent that day on the picket line. After pressure *The*

Guardian, Daily Telegraph and *Sun* printed tiny 'corrections' the same week. *The Times* did not do so until August. The *Standard* simply refused to 'correct' its lie.

In November Fryston colliery scab miner Michael Fletcher became a media 'hero' for allegedly being beaten up by striking miners. His bed in a Pontefract hospital was surrounded by hacks. After being sent home for the weekend, he returned to the hospital to star in a stage-managed visit from MacGregor for the benefit of the media. In the same hospital Charles Maxwell lay injured and ignored by these hacks. Maxwell, a striking miner from the same pit, was beaten to the ground on 20 November by 5 police thugs. He spent 4 days in hospital with kidney, back and facial injuries.

A month earlier wheelchair-bound Brenda Stout was viciously attacked in her own home by three masked scabs; she was slapped, slashed with a knife, throttled with telephone cord and her home wrecked. The attack was described by the police as 'half-hearted'. It was largely ignored by the media. Brenda Stout is a member of the Bickershaw Wives Support Group.

When the home of a scab miner was destroyed by fire, the media waxed eloquent about 'arson'. The man concerned had burnt his home himself. When a scab miner appeared on television with his face scarred by acid, the cliché books were rifled for phrases of condemnation. This man was later found to have done it himself for publicity. Publicity was willingly given by the bought-off media.

The emergence of working class women as an independent political force in the strike has frightened the life out of the ruling class. Consequently the women are belittled, patronised or ignored by the media. Stories about women in soup kitchens are just about acceptable. Working class women as political fighters, organisers, picketers and resisters of police violence – such stories are not acceptable. Thus the 10,000 strong women's march in Barnsley and 20,000 strong women's march in London were largely ignored. What would have been the media response if 10,000 women had marched *against* the strike?

The miners' strike has exposed more sharply than ever the myth of a 'free' press and 'independent' broadcasting. The media are owned by the ruling class to serve the interests of the ruling class. Three rich men – Robert Maxwell, Rupert Murdoch, Victor Matthews – own 75% of all daily and 83% of all Sunday papers sold. Tiny Rowland of Lonrho 'freely' bought *The Observer* to protect his profiteering and theft in Africa. Two companies – W H Smith and Menzies – control newspaper and magazine distribution to over 80% of newsagents. The media are as much part of the capitalist state as courts and cops. The media lie is as much a weapon against the working class and oppressed as the police truncheon.

It is equally true that media workers who disseminate anti-NUM propaganda are as much strike-breakers as scab miners who cross picket lines. Despite the whining that breaks out from time to time about 'media bias' media workers, with a few honourable exceptions, have continued to disseminate anti-strike material. Yet distributing a media lie is as treacherous as moving coal from a pithead. Media trade unionists who support the miners' strike should refuse to handle anti-strike material just as some transport workers have refused to handle coal. This would not only be real solidarity with the miners but also a real blow against the ruling class lie-machine deceitfully called the 'free' press.

TERRY O'HALLORAN
January 1985
Thanks to Campaign for Press and Broadcasting Freedom for information supplied.

Fitzwilliam 9 Trial

'I am the judge and the jury'. These were the words spoken by the stipendiary magistrate as he convicted seven of the Fitzwilliam 9, imprisoning Peter Hurst. The 9 were charged in connection with the incidents on 9 July when police stormed into the mining village of Fitzwilliam wreaking havoc in their wake. He said that this was a 'perfectly lawful operation' – a lawful operation that left three people needing hospital attention, one of whom was detained for three days, and another overnight with a head injury.

The trial in Pontefract Magistrates Court lasted two weeks, finishing on 14 December 1984. The evidence put forward by the prosecution was on a political theme when questioning the defendants. The prosecutor asked them: 'Are you a member of any political organisation?'; 'Do you go picketing?'; 'Were you at Orgreave?'; 'Are you a member of the NUM?'; 'Do you attend political meetings?'. He thus attempted to paint a picture of political subversion – a picture that the magistrate wished him to supply.

The defending counsels, Lord Gifford, Henry Spooner and Patrick Healey found massive contradictions in the police evidence. During cross examination:

● the police were asked how was it that when the police came under a hail of missiles from 9.30pm to 11.15pm that night, no police officer was hit, and that only one was injured.

● they were also asked to account for 15 truncheon marks on one defendant's back, when the police concerned claimed that he was struck seven times on the front of his body. No marks were found on the front of his body. Medical evidence supported the theory that the defendant was restrained and thoroughly beaten by a number of assailants.

● one police officer claimed that it was normal procedure to transfer a prisoner from one van to another by the hair, despite being handcuffed.

● one police officer's notebook was doctored to corroborate evidence given against Peter Hurst.

After all this the magistrate sentenced as follows: *Peter Hurst* – six months imprisonment for threatening behaviour!; *Allen Hurst, Brendan Conway and Peter Doody* – four months suspended for two years; *Joenne Worth, Mary Ball and Lee Morris* – bailed whilst social enquiry reports are made; *Denis Doody, Brian Linley* – acquitted. After the trial a press conference was called by FRFI and LPYS to tell the truth about 9 July.

We regard the sentence on Peter Hurst as a heartless and cruel deed. Both his wife and two young children are without a husband and father over the period of Xmas. We feel this deed is befitting the type of society in which we live – oppose the state and you are immediately criminalised.

Lord Gifford remarked to an officer under cross-examination, 'you have no regard for either truth or accuracy', and in our opinion neither did the stipendiary magistrate. He took the side of his employers, the state. He had every intention of assisting his masters in repressing a section of the working class now engaged in struggle against British imperialism. This type of action against our community will not serve to subdue us, it will only harden our resolve to overcome our enemy the present state. We call for all readers to support the struggle of the NUM and the struggle of Peter Hurst and the 150 other miners in Armley Prison, Leeds at the moment and the comrades of Hemsworth and Fitzwilliam. A support group is being set up in Fitzwilliam by the relatives and by FRFI to defend the prisoners and to make sure they don't stand alone. It will be organising aid for the families, protests and support for the prisoners.

DENIS

Scotland goes out to the people!

'Go Out to the People!' was the rallying call of Scottish FRFI's weekend of action in solidarity with the miners; and that was just what we did. On Saturday 23 February about 50 people assembled in Dundee City Square from Dundee, Edinburgh and Glasgow, prepared for all-out activity to build support for the miners. Two Yorkshire miners also travelled up from Fitzwilliam to tell the people of Dundee about the Prisoners Aid Committee which had been set up to defend the hundreds of miners who are now being sent to prison. Collections took place all over Dundee, both in the city centre and in working class areas. About 40 people attended the Sunday Dayschool.

The tour by the Fitzwilliam miners around the Weekend of Action to Dundee, Edinburgh, Glasgow and Fife was a major step forward for all those working for the miners' cause. Seeds have been sown which now need the hard work of dedicated people if the ideas are to be carried through. FRFI will be in the centre of this.

HELEN ANDERSON

Paul Mattsson

Islington out on the streets

'We live in hard times which demand a hard response from a hard left...what is needed is a hard left of principled people prepared to support those in struggle.'

Tony Benn's speech to the 1,500 strong demonstration in Islington on 19 January brought into focus all the lessons of the strike for miners and for all those who support their struggle. He told the crowd: 'Don't wait for permission. If you wait for permission you'll wait forever!'.

Benn described the work done in his constituency in Chesterfield where a Community Defence Committee had been set up comprising women's groups, trade unions, Labour Party branches, the CPGB, the NCCL and even members of the clergy. They are working to link the miners' struggle with every other struggle – they are organising for a one-day stoppage on the buses with a miner on every bus to explain their case; they want the schools opened up to the miners and to the unemployed as well. They held a party in Chesterfield to welcome home miners who had served prison sentences for the strike.

Pat, of Fitzwilliam Prisoners Aid Committee, was given a tremendous reception for her first public speech: '...the young miner who was intended to speak here today can no longer do so...he is now languishing in prison after being arrested yesterday morning for allegedly breaking his curfew...Who the bloody hell are they to tell people what time to leave here and what time to go there...Yes, these so-called lovers of freedom, democracy, the rights of the individual, that they are always preaching about. They are criminalising people who stand up for their democratic rights, the right to work, the right to travel the highway, the very right of basic human dignity is under serious threat from the present dictatorship in Number Ten'.

BUILD MINERS SUPPORT IN THE COMMUNITY

The demonstration was built in only a few weeks of hectic activity – every organisation, campaign, local support group was contacted, door to door and street leafleting done with collections and sales of the paper and by fly-posting every available wall. Local activists, including FRFI, were instrumental in this process. The turn out was worth every bit of effort – people and banners turned up from every part of London, miners' contingents with their colourful banners came, and local people joined in.

The FRFI contingent doubled in number as it shouted and sang through the working class streets – 'Whose riot? Police Riot', 'What do we want? Miners out of gaol! When do we want it? Now!' got the whole-hearted approval of miners in front of and passers by. Contingents from Irish Solidarity Committees and from the City of London Anti-Apartheid Group, plus those of the Nicaragua Solidarity Campaign and the Namibia Support Committee brought home the need for internationalism in all struggles today. A message of support and encouragement from Nicaraguan miners to British miners was read out and David Kitson, recently released from 20 years in South African prisons, praised the British miners and reminded everyone of the way the apartheid state and British support for it oppressed the miners of South Africa.

Annie Cooper, a miner's daughter and wife from Kent, had this to say about the needs of the struggle:

'What do the rich know about living from wage packet to wage packet? From Giro to Giro? Thousands have been arrested because they want to work, hundreds have been jailed for wanting to work...the money helps us to survive but not to win. We need action! Forward to 1985.'

The FRFI speaker called for demonstrations, pickets and rallies like this to be organised, winning the support from the thousands of unemployed, black people, Irish people, women and all fighting workers in struggle if the working class is to go forward. She called for support for the class war prisoners to be organised. An FRFI supporter, an NUT representative speaking on behalf of members at her school, stressed the need for more activities on the streets so that trade unionists could come out and show their support.

Trade unionists had come out – Islington Trades Council and NALGO – a branch of the GMWU, and Finsbury Park NUR plus NUT members from several schools. But despite the exhortations of the many Trotskyist group to the miners to organise this mass picket and that general strike, the majority of these left organisations could not organise themselves to bring a banner. The people will not wait for permission from the SWP, the WRP, RCP and others – they will demonstrate and organise when the call is made.

Thirty people signed up to join in the work of the Support Group when the call was made by Maggie in the collection speech – when she demanded not just money but every possible contribution from everyone there – whether in an organisation, trade union, tenants' group or as an individual.

GO OUT AND ORGANISE

FRFI and other activists who built the march are determined to take the struggle forward with as many people as possible – with rallies, street meetings, benefits, collections and pickets to build the support among the people.

ALAN JAMES AND MAGGIE MELLON

116

H-Block solidarity with the miners

Although I have previously expressed a personal message of solidarity with the struggle of the miners to protect their jobs, pits and communities, I would like, through *Fight Racism! Fight Imperialism!* to convey my admiration and encouragement to all those who have so courageously withstood all attempts to make them crawl before the 'would-be-masters'. Over the past year we Republican POWs have watched with a special interest the events involving the striking miners and a close affinity has been built up with those in the forefront of that struggle – much to the puzzlement of some in this country.

It is not merely a wish to see just anyone oppose Thatcher and the Tory government, regardless of who they are, but a genuine feeling of solidarity with people who we see experiencing a very similar situation as that in which we Irish Republicans exist. Particularly so in relation to the prison struggle – it is much more than coincidence that there are numerous similarities between events involving us and those which the miners have faced. Then if we examine the struggles waged by oppressed peoples throughout the world we learn that though the names and faces may change the underlying forces and factors which shape events are practically identical.

I mentioned earlier that our identification with the miners' plight has puzzled some – I was of course referring to those in British army uniform who walk our streets and help maintain imperialist oppression of our people. In many instances they themselves have families, relatives, neighbours and friends involved in the NUM strike and the sight of seeing those who they are meant to harass, oppress and

murder, if given the opportunity, collecting money, food-parcels etc for the relief of miners' families, comes as something of a shock to them. There are others no doubt of Irish origin who also wonder why we should be in any way concerned about 'those who are all the same, whose people are over here murdering us' – There are of course racists to be found everywhere and those who haven't seriously analysed the conflict here nor truly identified the real enemy.

In the rare television programmes which genuinely investigated events connected with the strike we had the opportunity of hearing striking miners and their families make reference to Ireland and how their views regarding the war being waged here had changed. They spoke of how they initially had been horrified and shocked at the sheer brutality of the police (sent to their villages to protect 'private property' and to ensure that those who 'sold their souls' – or who simply had never had one – would be protected as they carried out their scab activities) and they could now better understand events in the Six Counties. Normally such brutal and murderous actions of state forces were reserved for the peoples of England's colonies and it must say something for the crisis within capitalism, and England's decline as an imperial power, that she must today resort to such activities against her own people.

Unfortunately the vast majority of the labour force has not recognised this, or if they have, they have conveniently chosen to ignore it. But I'm sure it's wrong to simply blame the rank-and-file of the labour movement – at all times it is they who are the most militant and determined to protect their interests and rights, but their spirit of resistance has been gradually undermined and weakened by a leadership subservient to the ruling class – a leadership where selfish concern for their own prestige and position has blinded them to what the original aims of trade unionism were. In Ireland such people were once referred to as 'Gombeen men', lackeys, and history shows us that all oppressed peoples were cursed with such elements.

From our position in the H Blocks of Long Kesh we can easily understand the feelings of treachery and loneliness the strikers must have felt when all the rhetoric and verbalism, risen to such heights at the Labour Party and Trades Union congresses, never materialised into practical support and solidarity on the ground. We too once believed that 'nationalist' politicians who made much noise in support of our cause actually meant what they said, and it was a lesson to us when we discovered that beyond the rhetoric there was nothing. What we did discover though was that there were thousands upon thousands of ordinary people the length and breadth of Ireland, and in many countries throughout the world, who were at one with us in our struggle and who sought that victory just as ardently. Hopefully the miners and their families and communities will also be aware that there are those throughout the world, totally unconnected with the NUM strike, who seek victory for them just as much as they themselves do. Bobby Sands said when he knew he was shortly to die, ' . . . I die, not just in an attempt to end the barbarity of H Block and win back the rightful recognition as a political prisoner but because what is lost in here is lost for the Republic and those wretched oppressed whom I am deeply proud to know as the risen people . . . ' Likewise, what is lost in the coalfields of Kent, Yorkshire, Wales is lost for the people of West Belfast, Derry, the Six Counties, El Salvador, Chile, Peru . . . and

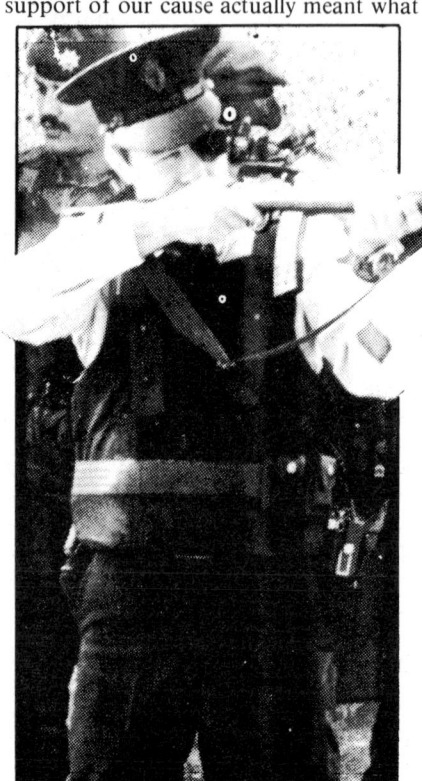

what is won in these places is won for the working class, property-less peoples of the world.

The media's portrayal of the strike surpassed even my own expectations as to how blatantly partisan they can be and no one should any longer be in any doubt (if ever anyone was!) that they are merely another tool in the hands of the ruling class. For many months we were treated to the spectacle of 'picket violence' with loud condemnations from all-round; even Kinnock had to have his tuppenceworth. But once numbers returning to work rose to sufficient levels the 'violence' mysteriously disappeared from our screens and each evening of news was how many 'went back to work that day'.

We POWs experienced a similar portrayal of our prison struggle though in reverse order. With the beginning of the 'blanket protest' (well documented in

118

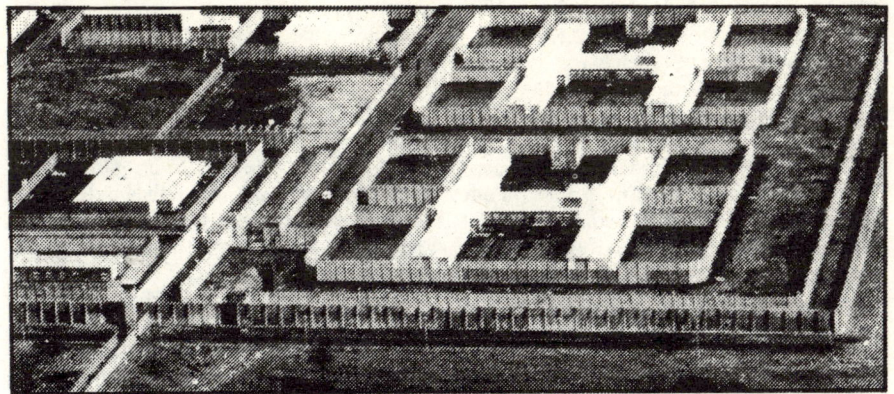

Photo: H-Blocks, Long Kesh concentration camp

David Reed's book, *Ireland: the key to the British revolution*), the evening news daily gave the figures of those in the H Blocks 'conforming' to prison rules and those not. At one stage it rose to about 90 conforming and 10 not – the only thing they neglected to mention was that the 90 were a mixture of loyalists and non-political prisoners while only the 10 were Republicans! Gradually more Republicans were sentenced and the 10 became 20, then 30, 40, 50 – until the figures suddenly dropped from the news; obviously they had become too embarrassing to the Northern Ireland Office (NIO). Later came the 'violence' of the no-wash protest (a totally passive protest of non-cooperation with prison staff) and later still the 'violence' of the hunger-strike. Paradoxically, the same media refer to Gandhi's hunger-strike as a 'supreme form of passive protest'.

One major result of the miners' strike has been the politicisation of the rank-and-file workers, and just as importantly, and even more so, the involvement of the women in the struggle. Those mothers, wives, sisters who probably once thought they would never be involved in political work, never mind being to the forefront of such a militant and revolutionary struggle, have earned the respect and admiration of not only their own families and com-munities but oppressed peoples everywhere. Our own female comrades, friends and relatives showed the same revolutionary capabilities in the Relatives Action Committees formed during the period of our prison protest. It wasn't that they suddenly created these capabilities – they always had them. But they now were given the opportunity to use them. Our imprisoned comrades in Armagh prison must be an example to all women wherever they may be. Though small in number they have shown those who thought to intimidate, degrade and brutalise them, that once one has a conviction, a committment to a struggle for freedom from whatever oppression, then no might of the aggressor will defeat them. As Republican POWs we salute the courage and total selfless dedication of the women of the coalfields.

With the decision to initiate an 'organised return to work' there will doubtless be a certain amount of demoralisation amongst those who gave so much to the NUM struggle over the past year and who will question if it was all for nothing. While not presuming to be in a position to give those people advice as to what they should or shouldn't do, I would again refer to the course of our own prison struggle – a struggle which I feel bears so many striking similarities to that of the NUM – and ask those miners to look and see if they can find any encouragement from it.

From the start of our prison protest in

119

1976 to the end of the hunger-strike in 1981 our hopes had, in the intervening period, at times soared to great heights only to be then dashed almost to despair. Many various and prolonged attempts were made to break us and even our families were not spared from this. Prominent political activists who organised support groups on our behalf were even murdered by Loyalist death-squads on the orders of British intelligence (as was revealed in court by those tried for the murders). Finally 10 of our comrades died on hunger-strike in an attempt to achieve our objective – the recognition and rights of political prisoners. Our demands were not something far-fetched – we merely (like the NUM) wanted the British government to stand by the agreement made in 1972 when they first granted political status to Republican POWs.

What oppressors throughout history have failed to learn however is that by the mere fact of 'winning' a battle they have often lost the war. General Westmoreland still claims to this day, which is probably correct, that the American armed forces never lost a battle against the Vietcong; they did however lose the war, and while Margaret Thatcher may have claimed to have 'won' the hunger-strike battle the very fact that it had ever taken place showed the world that Republican prisoners were indeed political prisoners. Apart from that, the lessons learned and experience gained through that five year period of protest were to contribute greatly both to internal military victories and external political ones.

With the unsuccessful conclusion to the hunger-strike there was of course a general demoralisation felt amongst the POWs, but this did not last long. Years of struggle had taught us to be resilient and it was merely a question of analysing our position and formulating strategies. One year later (October 1982) a decision was made to end the 'no work' protest and thus be moved into all the H Blocks (we had until then been isolated in two of the eight H Blocks),

not to give up our struggle for our demands but to once again be amongst all the prisoners and to initiate a campaign for segregation from Loyalists. Isolated in small numbers we had been more easily controlled.

Less than one year later – on September 25 1983 – 38 Republican Prisoners drove out the front gate of the prison and so happened the greatest escape in the history of British prisons. The supposedly 'defeated and demoralised' had shown that defeat in a battle only means total defeat in the war if you allow it to be – the revolutionary however merely redirects his/her energies into another course of action. Shortly after this the NIO also had to accept that the integration of Loyalist *and* Republican prisoners was unworkable and segregation had to be conceded – we had won another battle.

I don't mean to boast of our actions but hopefully to show those miners who have struggled so hard that the end of the strike does not necessarily mean the end of the struggle for their demands. Rather they have shown all people what can be achieved when they unite together in common cause and have raised the consciousness of their own people and others in a way which could never be equalised by any amount of political theorising.

I would hope also that the people of the mining communities now feel a solidarity with other oppressed groupings in their own country and with oppressed peoples in other lands – particularly my own country.

Some glaring contradictions have certainly come to the fore and many inconsistencies on the part of those who supposedly represent the interests of the working class in England. Many of those contradictions and inconsistencies had been apparent to us long before now – not because we are more politically aware than others – but because we bore the brunt of those contradictions. The Secretary of State for the Six Counties who was most infatuated with the desire to achieve a military defeat of the IRA and whose 'Green light' to the SAS and other undercover operatives led to the deaths of many civilians as well as IRA volunteers, was none other than the NUM-sponsored Labour MP – Roy Mason! The fact that a so-called representative of the working class still has to have a numerous and ever-present bodyguard to protect him from the revenge of an oppressed people says a lot for the working class leadership I referred to earlier. I do accept however that there are notable exceptions – amongst those of course being the NUM President Arthur Scargill.

Marx had a means of testing the depth of his contemporaries' revolutionary views which was by questioning them on various international issues and from the answers they gave deciding as to whether or not he considered them to be truly revolutionary in their thinking and practices in the art of socialist thinking. It was a personal interest of his to expose the Roy Masons of his day!

In conclusion, I would like to thank *Fight Racism! Fight Imperialism!* for the opportunity to express my views on the NUM struggle. I would also like to thank them for the copies they freely provide to us, for the time, energy and finance they have expended on behalf of imprisoned Republicans in English prisons. I believe the views I have expressed in my letter are also those of my imprisoned comrades and if good wishes and feelings of solidarity had been enough to achieve victory then those emanating from the H Blocks of Long Kesh directed towards the striking miners, their families and communities would have defeated MacGregor, Thatcher and the Tories ages ago. As POWs we have no more than good wishes and the hand of revolutionary solidarity and comradeship to extend to you but these we are more than glad to offer you.

Onwards—ever onwards to victory.

Tiocfaidh ár lá

LAURENCE MCKEOWN, H BLOCK 5.

121

REVIEW

Don't shout 'scab' shout 'scapegoat'

The Miners' Next Step, Revolutionary Communist Party (RCP) pamphlet by Frank Richards. Junius Publications 1984, pp52, 50p

It is fitting that a review in the *Financial Times*, no less, should have said of this pamphlet:

'In a well-argued pamphlet entitled the Miners' Next Step . . . they rip into the NUM's left leadership for collaboration in the Plan for Coal and take a relatively mild view of the working miners because they are merely following the logic of their leaders collaborationism'.

As the FT reviewer says, it is common for those on the left to attack trade union leaders:

' . . . but rarely from the same side of the barricades as the entire establishment.'

The RCP has however done precisely this. It has campaigned throughout the strike for a national ballot. In doing so it has joined the entire ruling class and opposed the wishes of the striking miners. This pamphlet explains how the RCP arrives at such an absurd position. Its method is simple – at all costs ignore reality.

The miners' strike has, more than any other trade union struggle, demonstrated the fundamental realities of working class struggle in this period. Firstly, the deep split in the working class movement with Notts miners scabbing, steel workers unloading scab coal and the reluctance of many other sections to aid the miners. Secondly, it has shown the ruthlessness with which the ruling class will resort to its

classic methods for dealing with working class opposition – police brutality, rigged courts and a vast apparatus of lies and brute force with which the rich sustain their power. The question of ruling class force is apparently of little interest to the RCP, since their pamphlet barely mentions the sustained attack which the striking miners have suffered. Instead it concentrates on what it calls 'disunity' but does so in order to deny that a fundamental division exists in the working class. For the RCP the Notts scabs are not scabs at all they are . . . 'scapegoats'.

Why are the majority of Notts miners working? Most striking miners explain it quite simply – greed. This simple explanation is not good enough for the RCP, who, being middle class, do not know that people are moved to fight or not to fight by very material considerations. For the RCP:

'There is no correlation between militancy and wage levels'.

Indeed the pamphlet rejects the fact that sections of the Notts miners are relatively privileged in comparison to miners in other regions where many more pits are threatened. Relying on a set of figures which show that in two areas of Yorkshire, miners earn higher bonuses than in Notts the RCP triumphantly proclaims that this:

' . . . explodes the myth of the labour aristocrats of Nottinghamshire'.

So why *are* they working?

'The Notts miners believe that the future of the mining industry can be better safeguarded through industrial peace rather than through strikes. The only (!) difference between Nottinghamshire and the other regions is that as a result of its peculiar experience, collaboration and sectionalism are more entrenched . . . '

So that's the only difference! Most of us thought the difference was that the scab Notts miners are on the side of the ruling class whilst the strikers are on the side of the working class. Piling absurdity on absurdity the RCP continues:

122

'In Nottinghamshire many miners look for solutions through cooperation with the Coal Board. In Scotland miners have learned that their future depends on fighting the Coal Board. Unfortunately both wings of the movement are politically tied to the Coal Board.'

Now we understand! It's not which side of the barricades you are on but what is in your head that counts. Hence the RCP's belief that the NUM's decision not to have a ballot was a:

'...refusal to campaign to win the arguments for strike action among the miners.'

Since no material causes underlie the decision of the Notts men to scab (or the steel workers to betray the miners) it is all a question of changing people's minds by rational argument. This is indeed the tea-party theory of class struggle. It reminds me of those British leftists who argue that the Six Counties loyalists can be rendered progressive by socialist agitation.

The rest of the pamphlet is the stock British left denunciation of the NUM leadership, in this case for sowing illusions in the Plan for Coal. Since Scargill's leadership of the strike has up to now been impressive, the RCP simply lies. Whilst the ruling class and the Labour Party leadership denounce the miners for using 'un-British' and 'untypical' methods, the RCP says the NUM leadership is 'running a routine trade union dispute'. 6,000 arrests? Two killed? Workers in gaol? Routine?

It is hard for idealists such as Frank Richards to realise that the lessons learnt by the miners as they have fought scabs, police and ruling class intimidation matter a hundred times more today than their views on the Plan for Coal. But I was forgetting a fundamental principle of middle class socialist politics: no workers can learn lessons without the intervention of arrogant British trotskyists. Can't you just picture the scene on the picket lines in Nottinghamshire, 'Now lads, don't shout scab, shout scapegoat ...'.

MAXINE WILLIAMS

REVIEW

State of Siege

State of Siege—Miners' Strike 1984. Politics and Policing in the Coal Fields. By Jim Coulter, Susan Miller and Martin Walker. Canary Press, 241pp, £3.50.

Denis, a striking Yorkshire miner, and Chas, a communist activist, review *State of Siege*, a new and comprehensive analysis of the police role in the miners' strike

This book is an extensive inquiry into the present miners' strike. It deals in graphic detail with the role that the state has played in mobilising every part of its apparatus to defeat the NUM. It is made up of three volumes written as the strike has developed – the titles of each section reflect the development of the attack on the NUM and most importantly the response of the miners and the women in the coalfields. From a *State of Siege,* to the *Iron Fist,* to *Agitate! Educate! Organise!*

NATIONAL POLICE FORCE

This book is prefaced by the state's intention to render picketing ineffective by the use of the law. As is well known, at the start of the strike, Nottinghamshire was under siege from the police – miners, and especially Yorkshire miners, were never allowed into the county. But before all this happened the state had been preparing. As a result of the defeat of local police at Saltley Gate in 1972, the National Reporting Centre was set up as a means of co-ordinating police operations on a national scale. The book exposes the intentions of the Association of Chief Police Officers and brings credence to the claims of there

123

being a national police force that can be mobilised by just a phone call.

IRELAND

It draws with great clarity comparisons with the policing in the Six Counties of Ireland. The book compares the scabs in Notts and the protection of their 'right to work' with the loyalists in the Six Counties and their so-called right to a separate sectarian state. What is more, right from the very start, the authors point to the fact that 'new allies' for the miners will be found amongst those who have already witnessed the gathering of state power – the Irish people, black people and the unemployed. For these people have been branded as criminals just as the miners have been. The repression that the state dishes out points to these political conclusions. During this strike, just as in Ireland, the police and the state have been developing a whole series of new laws and practices for future use – the new Police Act, the riot training, the use of the prisons, the courts, intimidation of whole communities. It is significant also that police experience gained against the black youth who rose up in anger against the police in 1981, has been applied against the miners.

WAR

The authors make it clear the police assaults are part of a total war against the people of the pit villages. An older miner describes the police riots in Fitzwilliam and Hemsworth as 'a calculated attack on the community'.

While the pro-scab media diverts attention, the courts and prisons are mobilised to isolate activists from fellow strikers. On the evidence of police lies, miners are fined, 'bound over' and imprisoned. In Yorkshire's Armley jail alone, 150 miners are on remand. The war, however, is being fought on two sides and increasingly people are saying that the strike cannot finish while people are in jail. As one miner says,

'I don't think that it would be right to go back until our prisoners are released. What ever the charges are, the men have been forced into the situation. We shouldn't go back without people coming out of prison.'

WOMEN

The book also records the active and decisive role women are playing in the strike. One is quoted as saying,

'The women are behind the men and are backing them – they're 100% ... The women are there now, its opened our eyes. They're not going to sit back and wash pots – they're going to get out and fight.'

Another comments that she will never go back to just working in the home,

'I want to carry on working in a woman's group. I'd like to do some work on apartheid or CND'.

There are also tributes to support received from women up and down the country, especially from Greenham Common. The strike has meant,

'Women have established themselves as a powerful political force for the present and the future, a force which is fired with the enthusiasm born out of injustice and which, now created, will never be defeated.'

State of Siege is a book which fires a warning shot over the bows of the working class movement. Through its eye-witness accounts of what has happened during the strike it highlights the readiness of the state to attempt to quell any form of working class resistance to repression by the state. It has some sinister and very serious connotations of things to come. Orgreave was a practice ground for 'future urban disturbances'.

DENIS AND CHAS

REVIEW

Scargill and the miners

Michael Crick, Penguin, 1984, £2.50

'It is only by politicising our membership that we will ever bring about the
irreversible shift towards socialism in
society.'
(Arthur Scargill, 1981)

Michael Crick's latest book, *Scargill and
the Miners*, is both interesting and inform-
ative. It deals with a brief history of the
NUM since the 1950s and also the present
dispute up until September 1984.

Between World War Two and the 1960s
the Yorkshire Area of the NUM was a
right-wing dominated union. Union officials were corrupt and involved in sell-outs
and wheelings and dealings with the NCB.
They abused their positions, living off
expenses and rigging ballots in favour of
their protegés. Crick deals graphically with
Scargill's power struggle during his early
days as a rank and file member of the
NUM, showing how he sought to overthrow the right wing. Much of the information can be found in a more concise history
of the union in Vic Allen's book *The Militancy of the the British Miners*. Scargill
had to fight against the right in the NUM
from the start – at 18 he was refused entry
to his own branch meeting by union officials. He was young, vocal and a threat to
the union officials' own privileges and
interests. He battled on though and at one
meeting all the union officials stood up and
walked out of the meeting as he spoke.

A lot has been made of Scargill's membership of the Young Communist League
and debates continue as to whether he was
in the CP. Much of this is irrelevant, but it
is clear that the YCL did provide a political
education and training which has helped
him to be where he is today. Eventually
Scargill helped initiate the 'Barnsley
Forum' which was a left-wing NUM splin-
ter group which sought to influence and
change the NUM policies and leadership.

Scargill's determination, workrate and
dedication helped to some extent to
achieve this end. Despite Crick's quotes
from union officials such as Don Baines
and Peter Tait, who were involved in the
union at the time of the Battle of Saltley
Gate, and who claim that Scargill's role has
been overestimated, the facts clearly show
that it was Scargill who led the pickets on
the ground. Crick cannot alter the fact that
Scargill was and is a brilliant strategist and
trade unionist. He fought consistently for
the interests of NUM members in the
strikes of the 1970s, when the left wing
officials campaigned to get their members
out. As compensation agent, Scargill
earned the respect of Yorkshire's miners.

Crick misunderstands, because of his
background, the way people react when
faced with the type of repression the miners
have been subjected to. He probably
believes that the miners should remain passive, whilst the state and the police mete
out violence on a scale that is commonplace within the Six Counties of Ireland.

One chapter of the book is devoted to a
stool pigeon and scab, called Chris Butcher. Crick appears to think of this man as
hero and symbol of democracy. The fact of
the matter is that Butcher (Silver Birch) is
nothing short of a manipulated cretin.
Crick gives some credit to Butcher for initiative, although it is clear that Butcher has
had as many advisers as Thatcher herself – plus the fact that there would probably be a few bob in the deal for Butcher
himself. Butcher or Birch was nothing
more than a purposely invented stool
pigeon for the use of all and sundry on the
Tory front.

Scargill, as a trade union leader, cannot
be vilified as the press like to do once the
facts are laid out. Michael Crick's book

shows the struggle and determination that Scargill went through to change the NUM from an organisation which was dominated by the likes of Lord Gormley, into an effective and progessive fighting trade union. Politically Scargill is years ahead of his colleagues and has taken up wider political issues. He was joined at Saltley Gate by Irish civil rights activists after an appeal for support had been made to a demonstration against Bloody Sunday in 1972, and he never shied away from such support. He led miners to the picket lines at Grunwicks and outside the hospitals. Also more recently he has argued the common interest of the miners and the unemployed. This strike has politicised many people which Scargill stated in 1981 is one step on the road to socialism. Much of this is due to the fact that Scargill throughout his work with the NUM, has kept the interests of the miners, and the working class as a whole, at the forefront of his mind. For a more accurate account of this we may well have to wait for Scargill himself to write it.

DENIS AND CHAS

REVIEW

The fight belongs to us all

'Women against pit closures' by Barnsley Women. Published by Barnsley Women Against Pit Closures. 44 pages, £1.50

'The coaches arrived: one, two, three they kept coming – thirty and then forty, thousands and thousands of women from all over the country. And they were as determined as us – and ready to march. It was a magnificent sight and feeling.' (Page 20, Women's rally in Barnsley, 12 May 1984).

This first mass demonstration of women signalled the arrival of a powerful new force in British politics – a fighting organisation of working class women who had taken to the streets under the banner of 'Women Against Pit Closures'. Sickened by the bias in the media, groups of miners' wives, girlfriends, relatives and friends began to organise right from the start of the strike in March. They were determined to show that *they* were not the hostile and reactionary wives so beloved of the media. The pamphlet tells how on the contrary, they were ready to stand and fight alongside the National Union of Mineworkers (NUM). Inspired initially by the example of women at Greenham, the women involved in the now eleven month long miners' strike have gone from strength to strength in defence of their communities. As in countless revolutionary struggles throughout the world, it has been the courage and resilience of the women which has sustained the strike.

FOOD KITCHENS

Largely independent of the millions of

pounds owned by the NUM, and without the back-up of its organisational apparatus, the women have shown endless invention and determination in providing daily food for hundreds of thousands of people for nearly a year. They have often taken direct action – such as the occupation of Labour halls and welfare clubs – to get premises to set up kitchens. They have raised funds, organised food collection and distribution, given advice on DHSS benefits, held demonstrations at electricity board offices and DHSS offices. Women cook as many as 500 meals a day on a single cooker. The women's organisation of communal eating and child care has enabled thousands of women to come out of their individual homes to play a full part in political life for the first time. The effect on the strike, as acknowledged by Arthur Scargill and all the miners, has been dramatic. In fact, so far, it has meant the difference between victory and defeat.

In addition to the NUM, women themselves have travelled up and down Britain and all over Europe to raise money. Most women have had no experience at all of public speaking, yet time and again they have forced themselves to do it for the sake of the struggle. As a result they have won thousands to support the miners' cause.

PICKETING

'At the beginning of the strike women from the Barnsley group wanted to go picketing and were told that it was a bad enough job organising the men. All I can say to that is women do not need anyone to organise them. They can organise themselves.' (Lorraine, Barnsley rally, 12 May 1984)

On the picket lines, women have proved very effective in turning back scabs – who have been too ashamed, on many occasions, to crawl past them. Police though, have not held back from being violent towards women. Many have been arrested, with one woman, Brenda Greenwood,

being held on remand in Risley Remand Centre, for breaking bail conditions. Anne Scargill, wife of NUM leader Arthur Scargill, who has played a major role in Women Against Pit Closures, was herself arrested for picketing and held for ten hours in police cells. In the pamphlet, Linda of Hood Green recounts the shock when a group of women who had been arrested, heard police referring to 'women prisoners'. 'Prisoners? Us? Yes, we suddenly realised that's what we were ... Our next ten hours together were going to be some of the longest ever. We were reprimanded for singing and making a noise ... '.

NATIONAL ORGANISATION

On 11 July a first national conference of women's groups was called which in turn called a national demonstration in London on 11 August 1984. Tens of thousands of women and their supporters turned up. There was singing all the way, police were jeered at every opportunity and a £45 million bill for lost DHSS benefits was presented to the DHSS headquarters. A permanent national office now exists at the NUM headquarters in Sheffield, and a second national delegate conference in November committed Women Against Pit Closures not only to winning the strike, but to carrying on to campaign on jobs, peace, health and education – particularly that of working class women.

PRISONERS

Perhaps the most urgent work that now faces women's groups, alongside that of maintaining food supplies, is work in support of miners who have been sent to gaol.

The British state has had decades of experience in criminalising those who oppose its rule. The techniques now being brought to bear on the mining communities, as many miners have now realised, are those perfected in the Six Counties of Ireland over the last fifteen years. If the British state uses its experience gained in Ireland, then so must we, too, find examples from Ireland in resistance to state terror. In the late 1970s in the Six Counties, mothers, wives and girlfriends of young Irish Republicans imprisoned in the H-Blocks of Long Kesh prison, formed Relatives Action Committees in support of the prisoners. Political status, previously granted by the Tory government, was withdrawn by a *Labour* government. In protest, many prisoners went 'on the blanket' – refused to wear prison clothes. A reign of unparalleled brutality and torture was launched against these prisoners. To the shame of the NUM, the Northern Ireland Secretary responsible was Roy Mason – Labour MP for Barnsley, sponsored by the NUM.

Lily Fitzsimons, mother of a young prisoner, said at the time to *Hands Off Ireland!* (an RCG magazine), 'The reason they're (the prisoners) refusing criminal status is because they're not criminals. They're prisoners of war ... As you know there's a struggle going on outside and the prisoners carry on the struggle inside.' The Relatives Action Committees spread – there were twelve in Belfast alone. They picketed embassies and government buildings, and built a mass movement on the streets. It is *only* the development of such a movement that can provide a challenge to the British state's treatment of the miners today. It is no surprise then that it is women in a South Yorkshire village, Fitzwilliam, that have taken the step of forming a Prisoners Aid Committee. Women – wives, girlfriends, daughters, mothers, friends of miners – will refuse to have them criminalised by the British state's courts and prisons.

Everyone should read this pamphlet.

OLIVIA ADAMSON AND MAGGIE MELLON

REVIEW

NCCL scabs on miners' strike

On 10 December the National Council for Civil Liberties published a report 'Civil Liberties and the Miners' Dispute' – the first report of an independent inquiry called for by last year's NCCL AGM. The terms of reference of this inquiry were very clearly laid out:

'To inquire into and thereby establish the fullest possible account and the civil liberties implications *of the role of the police, the police authorities and the criminal courts* in the events, arising from and relating to the NUM dispute, which began in March 1984.' (emphasis added. Report page i)

The report, however, has taken it upon itself, in defiance of its own terms of reference: to condemn 'picket violence'; to justify police action in support of scabs; to defend the 'right' to break strikes by crossing picket lines. These reactionary positions were gleefully reported by the media as another stick to beat the NUM with.

The heart of this reactionary stance appears in the section 'Individual Civil Liberties':

'We accept that freedom not to take part in a strike is as much a fundamental right as the right to strike.'

This nonsense ignores the reality, obvious to all oppressed people, that what is at stake in the class struggle is not the rights of individuals but the rights of one class against another; the rights of the exploited and oppressed majority of humanity against the 'rights' of the privileged robber minority ruling class. The working class cannot recognise any so-called 'right' to break strikes by crossing picket lines. To do so is to accept the 'right' of the ruling class to destroy jobs and communities, impose unemployment, poverty, racism and national oppression on the people in order to sustain its own endless lust for profit.

The job of the NCCL is to defend the rights of the exploited majority, not to defend the rule of the rich under the spurious guise of 'individual rights'. The scabs in the miners' ranks are not defending democracy, they are defending the ruling class. As such they are traitors to their class and deserve no protection from the consequence of their treachery.

The logical consequence of the NCCL's reactionary stance is to justify police violence or as the report more politely terms it 'firm action' (see page 13) to defend the right of scabs to scab and to prevent strikers from seeking to stop such scabbing. The report calls this 'enforcement of the law of the land' which it regards as a 'compelling argument' (page 11). It is, indeed, 'compelling' if your own privilege and luxury depend on the 'law' that the ruling class shall continue to rule.

The police barbarity being meted out to striking miners is as vicious and unrestrained as it is, precisely because miners and their communities have challenged the holy right of the God profit to destroy their jobs and communities. The only compulsion striking miners come across is the 'compelling argument' of the police truncheon, the snatch squad, the crooked court and the prison wall. The striking miners are entitled to the unqualified support of all who are genuinely concerned with the rights and interests of the people. In this shabby report the NCCL has joined the ranks of the government against the miners on strike.

TERRY O'HALLORAN

REVIEW

Miners' strike – an adverse shift for the SWP

The miners' strike and the struggle for socialism – Socialist Workers Party, 20p

' . . . 'Why four and a half million people on the dole? Why old people dying of cold? . . . Police treating people rough: coming in at six in the morning and frightening the children. Suddenly I said "My God, that's what's been happening to blacks for years"'.
Kate Whiteside of the newly formed National Co-ordinating Committee of Women's Action Groups. (*The Guardian* 19 February 1985)

This new political consciousness, gained by thousands of working class men and women during the twelve months long miners' strike, shows the path of future working class struggle.

It is a dramatic gain for the working class movement. Yet the Socialist Workers Party (SWP) can only see: 'a very real and adverse shift . . . in the balance of class forces.' (Hallas, *Socialist Worker* 2 February 1985). This gloom and defeatism can only be explained by the fact that the SWP, whilst dreaming of revolution, has actually placed its faith in the rotten structure of the Great British Labour and trade union movement.

In the face of an obvious split in the ranks of the NUM – a split that has been mirrored throughout the trade union movement – the SWP have retained a blind belief in the organised rank-and-file at the point of production. Their fantasies about the

129

path of future working class struggle have been destroyed by the harsh realities of the miners' strike but they refuse to abandon them. Now their plan for the future advocates an even narrower 'struggle for socialism' – a retreat even from the workplaces of the better-off working class into what they themselves describe as the 'shells' of Trades Councils and trade union branches – in order to rebuild them (Hallas).

For this reason the SWP pamphlet *The miners' strike and the struggle for socialism* can offer no lessons and no way forward. It is a mixture of general abstract truths about the ABCs of their socialism interspersed with shallow references to the miners' strike.

The author, Harman, patronises his readers with primary school lessons about the terrible power of the state and its organised attack on the mining communities: how the capitalist class exploits the working class, how the state acts in the interests of the ruling class and how only the working class can overthrow the rotten system of capitalism. All well and good – but how is this to be done? Apparently with the aid of an abstract general formula:

'...one of the most important truths about modern capitalist society: a united and militant working class is more powerful than the strongest of states. We can beat the state – if we build that unity and militancy' (page 10)

Unfortunately the real class struggle has little time or patience with abstract general truths. Far from being united, there is a fundamental split in the working class movement as the miners' strike has conclusively demonstrated.

The split in the working class movement is the most fundamental political feature of capitalism since the advent of imperialism. The split is not simply between the 'bureaucracy' and the rank-and-file but goes deep down into the ranks of the working class. Dockers, power and steel workers and sections of miners themselves – on the whole the better paid in more secure jobs – have scabbed on the miners' strike.

The TUC and Labour Party has scabbed on the strike not simply because its leaders are rotten and well-off but because the movement itself represents the interests of the better-off working class. It is their movement. Trade unions have refused to sacrifice their massive funds, buildings, newspapers, status and privilege for the miners' strike. Trade unionists in crucial areas have refused to risk any threat to their jobs and conditions in order to give the most basic solidarity to the miners' strike.

The SWP cannot accept this. Their world of the rotten bureaucracy and the fighting rank-and-file will simply not square with the reality of the miners' strike.

Inevitably in the pamphlet they attack Arthur Scargill:

'He has not spoken openly to the active strikers on the ground about the lethargy, the incompetence and the bureaucratic sabotage of so many of the officials under him. He has been like a general who refuses to appeal over the heads of incompetent officers to the rank-and-file soldiers below to wage the battle in the only way that can assure success' (page 12)

In the middle of the fiercest class-war battle for decades, the SWP wanted Scargill to launch a purge of NUM officials in a period when the ruling class was intent on isolating him as an unrepresentative extremist. When you lead no troops you can afford the luxury of armchair criticism.

Scargill however has to concern himself with the real balance of forces within the miners' strike. The NUM is not a revolutionary organisation, but a trade union with all the political limitations that that entails. Arthur Scargill cannot change this and neither can the SWP.

The reactionary consequences of the SWP's simplistic division between the bureaucracy and the rank-and-file is highlight-

130

ed when the SWP occasionally shifts to the international arena. They say the lead the miners and others should follow is that of the Polish Solidarnósc and, inevitably, its right wing leadership against the Polish socialist state.

'What Thatcher is doing in Britain is no different, in this respect to what General Jaruzelski did in Poland when he staged a military coup to smash the independent workers union, Solidarity . . .'. (page 3)

We remind Harman that whilst the British miners have struggled heroically for twelve months to prevent capitalist market forces driving them into destruction, Solidarnósc and its leaders support the reintroduction of these same market forces to make Polish industry 'efficient'. Harman's anti-soviet-ism is so extreme that he dismisses the full employment policies practised by the soc-ialist countries in spite of the world crisis, by arguing that it is only because of 'wages even lower than dole payments in the West' that workers can get jobs. Little wonder that he does not tell us of the financial and political support which Soviet trade unions have extended to the striking miners.

Thousands of ordinary people, many outside the organised trade union move-ment, have given material and financial support to the strike. The organised work-ing class movement has failed to give the active solidarity which could have led to a victory. Little wonder that this movement has been unable to lead and organise the massive popular support that exists for the miners on strike and against the Thatcher government. It is this popular support that has to be organised to continue the struggle after the miners' strike ends.

This way forward has no time for the reactionary defeatism of the SWP. The SWP can hide itself in the 'empty shells' of trade union branches and Trades Councils with the Militant and other Trotskyist sects. Real revolutionaries recognise that the historic and heroic struggle of the striking miners and their communities has begun the process of building the class organisations that can take us forward in the struggle for socialism.

MAGGIE MELLON AND DAVID REED